DATE DUE

LENIN

and the Russian Revolution
in World History

Titles *in World History*

LENIN

and the Russian Revolution in World History

Judith Edwards

Enslow Publishers, Inc.

40 Industrial Road   PO Box 38
Box 398   Aldershot
Berkeley Heights, NJ 07922   Hants GU12 6BP
USA   UK

http://www.enslow.com

C 1   2003   18.85

Library of Congress Cataloging-in-Publication Data
Edwards, Judith.
  Lenin and the Russian revolution in world history / Judith Edwards.
    p. cm. — (In world history)
Includes bibliographical references and index.
ISBN 0-7660-1464-9
  1. Soviet Union—History—Revolution, 1917–1921—Juvenile literature. 2.
Lenin, Vladimir Ilyich, 1870–1924—Juvenile literature. I. Title.
II. Series.
    DK265 .E37 2001
    947.084'1'092—dc21
                                                        00-011603

Printed in the United States of America

10 9 8 7 6 5 4 3 2 1

To Our Readers: We have done our best to make sure all Internet addresses in this
book were active and appropriate when we went to press. However, the author
and the publisher have no control over and assume no liability for the material
available on those Internet sites or on other Web sites they may link to. Any
comments or suggestions can be sent by e-mail to comments@enslow.com or to
the address on the back cover.

Illustration Credits: © Corel Corporation, p. 105; Enslow Publishers,
Inc., pp. 6, 10, 16, 64, 67; Library of Congress, pp. 9, 28, 36, 38, 57, 72,
78, 81, 84, 93, 96, 106, 110, 112, 113; Russian State Archive, p. 48.

Cover Illustration: Enslow Publishers, Inc., (Background Map); Library
of Congress (Lenin Portrait).

Every effort has been made to locate the copyright owners of all the photographs
used in this book. If due acknowledgment has not been made, we sincerely regret
the omission.

Contents

Russia, as it looked around the turn of the twentieth century.

Chapter 1

Revolution!

It was early afternoon on March 15, 1917, in Zurich, Switzerland. Vladimir Ilych Lenin had just finished lunch when his friend Moisei Bronsky threw open the door and shouted unbelievable news.[1] Russia had exploded in revolution! Lenin and his wife, Nadezdha Krupskaya, rushed outside to find a newspaper.

These exiles from the Russian government were not just concerned for their homeland. Lenin had spent sixteen years of his adult life either in exile, imprisoned, or away from Russia. He had spent those years writing, giving speeches, organizing political parties, and waiting eagerly for the day when there would be a revolt against the oppressive government of the Russian tsar (ruler).

Lenin had worked not just for revolution, but for the complete overthrow of the Russian government, which did not allow ordinary people any say in making the laws of the country. Lenin wanted to replace the tsar not with a democracy, but with a socialist system, soon to be called communism. He believed that a Communist government would put workers in control of their own destiny. Lenin insisted that these workers would be led by a small number of dedicated, professional revolutionaries. His own party, called the Bolsheviks, from the Russian word for "majority," would lead the way to this coming "dictatorship of the proletariat"—dictatorship of the workers.

Now the time had come, and Lenin was far from Russia. World War I was raging, and he would have to cross enemy territory—through Austria-Hungary or Germany—to get to the Russian capital. He had to reach St. Petersburg, which had been newly renamed Petrograd.

Lenin explored several options. Perhaps he could start his journey through France or Great Britain, rather than enemy countries. However, these countries, which were relying on Russia as an ally in the war, were not likely to help Lenin—an outspoken opponent of Russian participation in the war—return home.[2] Lenin considered all possible routes home, both practical and fantastical. The situation was critical. He had to return to Russia if he wanted the Bolsheviks to have the deciding influence in shaping the outcome of the revolution.

Germany—Russia's enemy in the ongoing war— was quite willing to help Lenin. The Germans knew all

Vladimir Lenin was a famous revolutionary in exile at the start of the Russian Revolution.

about Lenin's hatred of the tsarist government and his wish for Russia to lose the war so the government would fail. The Germans thought that transporting Russian revolutionaries like Lenin back to Russia just might help Germany win the war.

Secrecy was important. The Germans did not want their enemies to know what they were doing and try to stop them. Likewise, Lenin and his fellow Russian exiles did not want the Russian people to know that they were being helped by their German enemies.

Lenin, the Bolshevik leader the Germans wanted most to send back to Russia, would be permitted, through complex and devious negotiations, to choose those who would return to Russia with him. A sealed train would transport the revolutionaries. They would travel from Switzerland, across Germany, into Sweden, and then south through Finland to reach the Russian frontier.

When the thirty-two Russian exiles started out on this highly secret journey, they had no idea if they

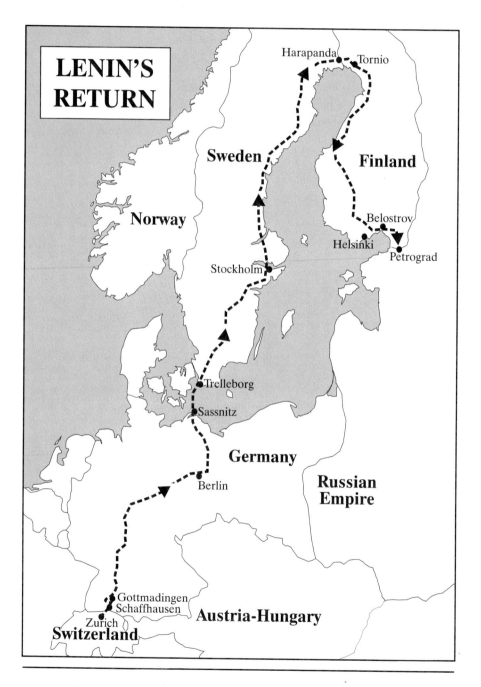

This map traces the route of Lenin's return to Russia in 1917.

would make it all the way back to Russia. Even if they did arrive, they could not be sure what kind of reception they would receive. Most of all, they were concerned about how the Provisional Government—which had recently been put in place temporarily to replace the tsar—and other revolutionary groups would feel about the return of the famous Vladimir Ilych Lenin.[3]

Chapter 2

Who Was Lenin?

In 1870, Simbirsk, the capital of the Russian province of Simbirsk, was a quiet town along the Volga River, east of Moscow. It was pretty in spring and summer, with flowers and fruit trees lining the riverbanks, but it became bleak in winter. In the late nineteenth century, Simbirsk was home to forty-three thousand people and the usual assortment of schools, churches, libraries, and businesses that make up a town.

Family Ties

The Ulyanov family was living comfortably in Simbirsk when Vladimir Ilych Ulyanov, the third of six children, was born on April 10, 1870. (His birthdate was April 10 on the old-style Julian calendar that Russia used at the time. On the more modern Gregorian calendar used by most other countries, his birthdate was April 22. Unless otherwise stated, all dates mentioned will follow the new-style calendar.)

Ilya Nikolayevich, the new baby's father, was a mathematics teacher and an inspector of schools for the ministry (department) of education. Ilya's father had been a tailor, the son of a serf. (Russian peasants, who were required to give part of their farm crop or any other earnings to the large landowners on whose land they lived, were called serfs.) Ilya's mother was Swedish.

As a child, Vladimir had very dark, slanting eyes; high cheekbones; and a broad, flat nose, all of which gave him an Asiatic appearance. In fact, his great-grandmother was Kalmyk, one of the Mongolian peoples who were accepted into greater Russia when they were baptized as Orthodox Christians. Vladimir's mother, Maria Alexandrovna, was the daughter of Alexander Blank, a German Jewish doctor who also became a baptized Christian. Becoming a Christian, no matter what one's original religion, was the only road to social and professional acceptance in Russia at the time. Dr. Blank married a German woman who was very well educated. He eventually bought a thousand-acre estate in Kokushkino.

The child Vladimir, who would later become the father of the Russian Revolution, was German, Swedish, and Kalmyk. According to historian Robert Payne, "There was not a drop of Russian blood in him."[1] Vladimir Ilych Ulyanov, who later called himself Lenin, had a family tree as diverse as any American's.

After the revolution, Lenin's family background would be covered up by Communist party leaders "because it was felt that the leader of the Russian revolution must be a Russian."[2]

School Days

As a small child, Vladimir had difficulty learning to walk, and sometimes threw tantrums. He had a bad habit of breaking things on purpose.[3] Even so, his quickness of mind and frequent sweetness made him a favorite at home.[4] He became an excellent student, particularly interested in languages.

When Vladimir's father was promoted to director of schools for the whole province of Simbirsk, the family moved to a larger home. It was a sunny house with many rooms that were filled with books and plants. Vladimir covered the walls of his room with maps.[5] Outside, there were orchards that held apple and cherry trees.

The Ulyanovs spent summers at their estate in Kokushkino in the province of Kazan. One fifth of the property was owned by Vladimir's mother, Maria Alexandrovna, and the rest by her siblings. Here, as well as in Simbirsk, Maria Alexandrovna enjoyed growing flowers with her children's help.[6]

The family had servants, including a private tutor who remained with the Ulyanovs until the children entered school around the age of nine. It was not unusual for children of well-off Russian people to enter school late. Private tutors and parents usually gave children their early education. The secondary school, which prepared students for examinations, was called a gymnasium. Upon entering the gymnasium, there was a wide selection of subjects to choose from and to learn in detail. Even before going to school, Vladimir had won a reputation as a hard worker.[7]

A boy who shared a desk with Vladimir said, "At school Ulyanov differed considerably from all of us, his comrades. Neither in the lower forms nor later did he take part in the childish and youthful games and pranks, always keeping to himself, busy either with his studies or some written work."[8]

The biggest influence on Vladimir was his older brother, Alexander. There were four years separating them. Alexander was very much the leader at home. He edited a family weekly newspaper to which he expected his four brothers and sisters to contribute.[9] Alexander was a brilliant student in school, especially interested in natural science. He was a generous and polite young man, who preferred to keep his private thoughts private. The young Vladimir adored him and tried to copy Alexander's even-tempered discipline.[10] The brothers were close during Lenin's early childhood, but their very different personalities had drawn them apart by the time Alexander left for college.

Death and Betrayal

The happy provincial life of the Ulyanov family ended abruptly with two incidents. First, Lenin's father, Ilya Ulyanov, died unexpectedly in January 1886, when

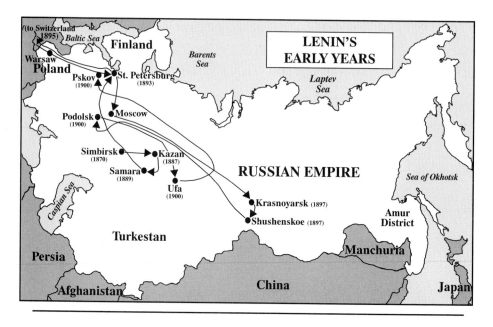

This map shows the places Lenin knew as a young man, and traces some of his early travels.

Lenin was just fifteen years old. Because he had been removed from his post as director of schools with no explanation the previous year, the father had not left much money behind. Maria Alexandrovna Ulyanova had to apply to the state for a pension, which was granted on request to people who worked for the state service, to support her family.

A year later, Alexander, who was then a college student, was arrested and put on trial for plotting to assassinate the tsar. Despite the pleas of his mother, Alexander was executed. Vladimir and Alexander's sister Anna had been visiting Alexander when he was arrested. She was arrested, too, but was released after

Alexander's execution. She was told, however, that she would be watched by the police and would have to move to the family estate at Kokushkino. The Ulyanov family, in Simbirsk, was shunned by neighbors.

This was a shocking and terrible blow to the family. None of the Ulyanovs had known that Alexander, the gentle and gifted student who had received a gold medal for outstanding work when he graduated high school, was involved in revolutionary activity.[11] For Vladimir, life would never be the same.

Chapter 3

Groundwork for Revolution

In Russia in 1887, there was no freedom of speech or freedom of assembly, liberties we take for granted in the United States. The tsar, equivalent to a king, was the absolute ruler of the nation. Though the tsar had popular support from the masses in Russia, events of the past century had created a class of intellectuals who were challenging the tsar's position of power and the effects it had on the people of Russia.

Development of Russia

Russia developed at a different rate and along different lines compared to Western Europe. The Russian Empire ranged across two continents—from the Gulf of Finland in the west and east to the Pacific Ocean; from the frozen Arctic in the north and south to the borders of what were then Turkey, Persia, and Afghanistan.

This empire was larger than the ancient Roman Empire at its peak. It comprised 8.5 million square miles, or one sixth of the total land surface of the earth.

Feudalism—the system based on the relationship between landowners and the peasants who lived on their land—was slow to emerge in Russia. This was because of the vast expanse of free land and the many different ethnic groups. The development toward modern culture also passed Russia by, mainly because Russia was not being used by other countries as a significant trade route by the thirteenth century. As a result, while the great art and new ideas of the Renaissance were flourishing in Western Europe, Russia remained isolated.

When the Mongols and Tatars (Asian peoples) invaded Russia during the thirteenth and fourteenth centuries, the remaining trade centers were destroyed, but the invaders were able to govern large areas of land. The invaders were willing to tolerate local customs, religions, and governments—as long as the local rulers and military establishment were submissive to Mongol dominance and paid tribute.[1]

As the Mongols gradually faded from power, the Russian nobility acted on what it had learned from its conquerors about government administration. In 1640, after instituting the Ulozhenie law code, which made serfdom a legal category binding a class of people to the land on which they lived, Moscow was made a holy city. This move, which made Moscow the home of the head of state and military organizations, was done with the cooperation of the Russian Orthodox Church. From the capital at Moscow, the tsar now ruled absolutely across the vast empire.

Rulers and Serfs

The masses in Russia came to think of the tsar as their "father" and the system as their caretaker. Threats to the empire from countries in Western Europe continually strengthened loyalty to the state and the tsar. The serf system, which kept peasants from moving from province to province within Russia, also helped stabilize the empire. The tax collector and the army recruiter were better able to keep track of where to find each person. Each village was responsible collectively for its share of tax money and its quota of soldiers to be drafted for war. Serfdom was solidified in Russia at the very same time it was declining in England and France.

The great problem for Russia was that its rulers lacked the technique and the manpower to rule their huge Eurasian empire. Unlike the civil service systems of other countries, the Russian bureaucracy generally operated as "the personal staff of the monarch rather than as the civil service of the nation," according to historian Richard Pipes.[2]

The Feudal Empire

In the seventeenth century, Tsar Peter the Great decided Russia needed to catch up with the rest of Europe, culturally and militarily. To do this, he brought in industry and introduced European culture to his reluctant nobility, who rebelled at the changes as much as they dared. Peter's changes were made not to help the peasants, who were left no better off than before, but because of the needs of the state.[3]

Western ideas infiltrated and changed the Russian feudal empire over the next century. A few dozen officers, most of them major landowners, rebelled briefly in December 1825. They hoped to form a constitutional monarchy. Though this Decembrist Revolt was quickly suppressed by the military, it led the government to rely more heavily on a professional bureaucracy, lessening the influence of the nobility.

By the time Tsar Alexander II freed the serfs in 1861, Russia was no longer totally isolated from modern ideas. In response to these changes, the weakened landowners either became reactionary or joined the new intelligentsia—writers, professors, and students who wished to liberalize Russian laws.

Alexander II wanted not only to free the serfs but also to engage the intellectuals in helping to expand the state's European institutions. In 1864, Alexander created the *zemstva*, the Russian word for local government institutions. These were set up to help Russia end its feudal system. The zemstva increased political awareness among the landowners and hinted at the beginnings of a middle class. New jobs were created as Alexander sought to bring about greater responsibility among the people in charge of new government bodies. The tsar made changes in the system of law, in the universities, and in censorship. His aim was to create

Source Document

. . . Examining the condition of classes and professions comprising the state, We became convinced that the present state legislation favours the upper and middle classes, defines their obligations, rights, and privileges, but does not equally favour the serfs, so designated because in part from old laws and in part from custom they have been hereditarily subjected to the authority of landowners, who in turn were obligated to provide for their well-being. . . . The way was opened for an arbitrariness burdensome for the peasants and detrimental to their welfare, causing them to be indifferent to the improvement of their own existence. . . . [T]he serfs will receive in time the full rights of free rural inhabitants. . . . At the same time, they are granted the right to purchase their domicile, and, with the consent of the nobles, they may acquire in full ownership the arable lands and other properties which are allotted them for permanent use. Following such acquisition of full ownership of land, the peasants will be freed from their obligations to the nobles for the land thus purchased and will become free peasant landowners.[4]

In 1861, Tsar Alexander II made provisions to free the serfs from their traditional condition, in which they were forced to remain on and work the land of wealthy nobles.

a representative government, under the tsar's leadership. Not all Russians were happy about this—particularly nobles who stood to lose their hereditary titles.

The Beginning of Revolutionary Terrorism

Revolutionaries—including former nobles, students, and discouraged members of the civil service—turned to terrorism to hasten changes that would help the former serfs. Tsar Alexander II approved a constitution on March 1, 1881. That same day, before it could take effect, he was assassinated.

Alexander II's son, Tsar Alexander III, returned to the strict line against political expression and independent social activity that had been the rule under his father's reign. At the same time, he wanted to continue Russia's modernization and industrialization. As usual when reforms came to tsarist Russia, peasants were the last to benefit from them. The authority of landowners was replaced by communes. Peasants were given plots of land that were partially owned by the state on which to grow crops. The communes were extremely inefficient. In order to be fair in distributing the limited land within each commune, historian W. Bruce Lincoln explained,

> peasant communes divided their holdings into many small strips according to the land's fertility, water supply, and distance from the village, and then assigned to every household the use of a certain number of strips depending upon how many holdings of each family thus lay scattered over the commune's entire domain.[5]

This system meant that farm tools had to be moved from strip to strip, wasting valuable time. Another problem was that the amount of land allotted to each family changed as the number of family members grew or diminished. Since many families had members die or leave to try the slowly growing industrial work in the cities, there was often not enough land for the peasants to produce their own food. And because they did not really own the land, there was no incentive to improve it. The soil was often ruined when it was used too many times for the same crop.

As the peasant's lot worsened, so did the repression of intellectual thought. Instead of continuing the permissive climate Alexander II had created for intellectuals, there was new censorship, particularly of students. Demonstrations were not allowed, and the police, who had allowed assembly during the reign of Alexander II, were active again in ending public political gatherings.

But the gates had already been thrown open. Democratic ideas were filtering through, even to partially educated Russians. The idea of revolution had been planted.

Conspiracy

Into this climate came the idealistic student Alexander Ulyanov. This older brother of Vladimir Ulyanov had, at first, ignored the attempts of other students to get him involved in revolutionary activity. In fact, the moderately well-organized revolutionary movement that brought about the assassination of Alexander II had been virtually wiped out by the time Alexander Ulyanov was a college student. Eventually, however, he became involved in a small—and very ineffectual— plot to assassinate Tsar Alexander III. Alexander Ulyanov became the revolutionary group's chief maker of explosives. When they were arrested, several of the conspirators lied about their involvement or renounced their cause to receive lighter sentences. Alexander, true to his honest nature, told his judges: "There is no finer death than death for one's country's sake; such a death holds no terror for sincere and honest men. I had but one aim: to help the unfortunate Russian people."[6] Alexander Ulyanov was put to death for his crime.

Chapter 4

The Making of a Revolutionary

One month after Alexander's execution, Vladimir Ulyanov graduated from high school at the head of his class. Alexander Kerensky, the director of the school, awarded Vladimir the gold medal, knowing full well that this would be noticed, given the recent execution of his brother. Kerensky gave Vladimir a glowing report, praising his dedication to his studies, and commented on his reserved character and isolation. He recommended Vladimir to Kazan University, one hundred fifty miles north of Simbirsk. Vladimir's father had gone to college there. It was an out-of-the-way school that generally serviced the minor nobility. Perhaps here Vladimir could excel in history and languages, and at the same time, get away from the stigma his brother's revolutionary activity had given the family.

College Student

Alexander's death affected Vladimir deeply. There is no proof, however, as some writers have suggested, that he became "Lenin the revolutionary" then and there. He did choose law and political economy as his major subjects, which immediately put him in touch with any revolutionary activity that might exist at Kazan. But even when he met informally with other law students, he was watched by the authorities.[1] Vladimir Ulyanov was present during a minor demonstration by students, though he was not actually seen to participate. Nevertheless, the fact that he was Alexander's brother led to his expulsion from Kazan. Not only was he expelled, but he was, like his sister Anna, confined to the family estate at Kokushkino.

If the authorities had thought about it, they might have realized that expelling this bright student just because his brother had been executed for revolutionary activity might have made it even more likely that Vladimir would become a revolutionary. "By thus ostracizing him, the tsarist authorities were steadily narrowing Lenin's range of choices. His solidarity with his dead brother became more firmly fixed," according to historian Dmitri Volkogonov.[2]

Both Lenin—a name he would adopt permanently in 1901—and his mother wrote respectful letters to the school authorities, trying to get him reinstated at Kazan. They were unsuccessful. Lenin also wrote letters requesting permission to attend a foreign university. These requests, too, were denied.

Lenin's early experiences influenced his development into the fierce revolutionary he later became.

Marxism

The family bought a small farm thirty miles from Kokushkino in 1889, in the province of Samara. Lenin completed his "exile" in this remote part of Russia, devoting himself to reading anything social and political. It was during this time that he first read Karl Marx's *Das Kapital*.

Karl Marx was a German Jew who believed in a classless society. He and his colleague, Friedrich Engels, believed that capitalism—the economic system in which businesses are owned and run by private individuals, leading to competition in a free market— allows business owners to exploit workers. Therefore, one class (the bourgeoisie, or middle-class business owners) oppresses another class (the proletariat, or workers). Because European countries (except for Russia) lived under this long accepted capitalist system, the only way to overthrow it and to win equality

Source Document

Let us now picture to ourselves, by way of change, a community of free individuals, carrying on their work with the means of production in common, in which the labour-power of all the different individuals is consciously applied as the combined labour-power of the community. . . . The total product of our community is a social product. One portion serves as fresh means of production and remains social. But another portion is consumed by the members as means of subsistence. A distribution of this portion amongst them is consequently necessary. The mode of this distribution will vary with the productive organisation of the community.[3]

Karl Marx believed that in a fully equal Communist society, people would produce as much food and other necessities as they were able, and would consume only what they needed. The community, or state, would be in charge of distributing goods to the people.

for all people, Marx argued, was by revolution—not by dialogue and laws, but by the forceful (if necessary) overthrow of capitalism.[4]

Marx taught that history showed that feudalism ended when power was taken from the ruling class of landowners and nobles by the capitalist middle class. The next stage of social change would come when the workers took power from the middle class. As Lenin read Marx's ideas, he realized that there was no real middle class in Russia. The tsar and those connected to him were still in power. Against whom, therefore, would the revolution be directed if it took place in Russia?[5]

A novelist named Nikolai Chernyshevski was very influential in shaping Lenin's interpretation of Marx. Of Chernyshevski's novel *What Is to Be Done?*, Lenin wrote, "It is a work that gives one a charge for a whole life." Two beliefs from this popular late-nineteenth-century book captured the mind of the extraordinarily disciplined young man whom the government had treated badly. According to historian Elyse Topalian, one was that "the individual is the potential holder of great power . . . that can influence events or even alter the course of history; and second, that total dedication to one's ideals means that any path toward achieving one's ends is valid and justifiable."[6]

Studies

While reading almost nonstop and absorbing new ideas that would, indeed, change the course of history, the young Lenin, not yet twenty-one, continued in his attempt to be reinstated at a university. Finally, thanks to his mother's efforts, Lenin was given permission to take the law examinations given by St. Petersburg University. He was allowed to study by himself and take the examinations when he felt ready.

Working intensively for a year at home—at a four-year college course in law—Lenin passed his exams with perfect grades. In November 1891, when Lenin was twenty-one, he received his diploma from St. Petersburg University. With a little more political wrangling from his mother, he was awarded the "Certificate of Loyalty and Good Character." Without this endorsement, he could not have practiced law, despite his first-class diploma.[7]

This amazing accomplishment, evidence of Lenin's intelligence and self-discipline, led to a disappointingly short and undistinguished legal career. In the years after getting his law degree, Lenin was really turning his attention to learning more about Marxism. He was gradually trying to be accepted as an important agitator in revolutionary circles.

Famine and Reform

At the same time Lenin earned his degree, the famine of 1891 started because of the policies of Tsar Alexander's finance minister, Ivan Vyshnegradskii. To increase Russia's gold reserves, the country had to create a better balance of trade with other countries. Since industrial growth had not managed to produce large amounts of marketable goods, Russia needed to export more food to achieve that trade balance. This food would come from the peasants who grew it. Vyshnegradskii proclaimed, "We may not eat enough, but we will export."[8] Because of his policies, whole villages starved. Then, an unusually severe winter in 1890–1891, followed by an unusually hot, dry summer, continued the disaster. Weakened by hunger, more of the rural peasant population was wiped out by disease.

This famine brought about a severe split in the viewpoints of those who were working for social reform. Georgi Plekhanov, a revolutionary leader who had been in exile from Russia since 1881, believed that bringing relief to famine victims only helped the government continue its poor management. He urged revolutionaries to use their energy instead to expose the weaknesses of the government, which would lead to its eventual overthrow. Moderates, on the other hand, argued that helping the government end the famine would lead to eventual reform, because it would increase the peasants' influence.

The early writings of Nikolai Chernyshevski and Plekhanov shaped the beliefs of the majority of young Marxists. Lenin's brother had been executed by the tsarist government, his family was shunned by the liberal intelligentsia, and Lenin had been denied the company of professors and fellow students during his college years. Though he read widely and formed his ideas not only from Marxist philosophers, Lenin was "never able to assimilate [take as his own] the ideas of the liberals, who proclaimed the rule of law, or the

Source Document

[L]et us examine more closely the case in which a man's own actions—past, present or future— seem to him entirely colored by necessity. We already know that such a man, regarding himself as a messenger of God, like Mohammed, as one chosen by ineluctable destiny, like Napoleon, or as the expression of the irresistible force of historical progress, like some of the public men in the 19th century, displays almost elemental strength of will, and sweeps from his path like a house of cards all the obstacles set up by the small-town Hamlets and Hamletkins. But this case interests us now from another angle, namely: When the consciousness of my lack of free will presents itself to me only in the form of the complete subjective and objective impossibility of acting differently from the way I am acting, and when, at the same time, my actions are to me the most desirable of all other possible actions, then in my mind necessity becomes identified with freedom and freedom with necessity; and then, I am unfree only in the sense that *I cannot disturb this identity between freedom and necessity*, I cannot oppose one to the other, *I cannot feel the restraint of necessity*. But such *a lack of freedom* is at the same time its fullest manifestation.[9]

Georgi Plekhanov was one of the foremost Russian thinkers in the years leading up to the Russian Revolution. His work had a strong influence on Lenin.

'Economists', who wanted the workers to flourish, or the Western democrats, who put parliamentary government above all else."[10] According to historian Dmitri Volkogonov, "For Lenin, Marxism meant above all one thing, and that was revolution. It was the revolutionary message of the doctrine that attracted him in the first place. . . . Lenin's 'discovery' of Marxism was thus extremely selective; he saw in it only what he wanted to see."[11]

In Siberia

The peasant masses, who were busy simply trying to avoid starvation, were not ready to listen to the revolutionary zeal of the self-proclaimed Russian Marxists, who were severely divided even among themselves. It was time to turn to urban workers—the proletariat—to continue illegal revolutionary organization.[1]

Lenin moved from Samara to St. Petersburg in the summer of 1893. Though Lenin worked in a law office, his main activity in St. Petersburg was organizing in Marxist circles. Even at legal meetings, he talked about Marxism. He was watched by the police. He continued to write and talk about his main themes from Marxism: "classes and class struggle, and the dictatorship of the proletariat."[2]

Lenin worked hard to achieve recognition as a revolutionary.

Meeting Other Marxists

Another revolutionary, Julius Tsderbaum, also called Yuli Martov, had arrived in St. Petersburg in 1893 after a short stint in prison for agitating. Lenin's association with Martov led to the formation of a dedicated Marxist group. In 1895, Lenin was granted a visa to go abroad. He made a brief visit to the Marxist leader in exile, Plekhanov. The famous revolutionary was impressed with Lenin's dedication.

Back in St. Petersburg, in addition to attending many secret Marxist meetings, Lenin and some of his colleagues began handing out Marxist propaganda in factories. He hoped that "this would bring them [the workers] in conflict with the state authorities and in this manner politicize them."[3] Lenin was disappointed in the workers' response. There was no freedom of speech in Russia, and the workers were reluctant to risk their jobs and their lives by going along with these revolutionary ideas.

Lenin himself was arrested in 1895 for his propaganda activity. He spent a year in prison in St. Petersburg.

There, he spent most of his time doing research for a book he would work on later. One of the people who supplied him with research materials was Nadezhda Krupskaya, a young Marxist teacher he had met while attending political meetings.

Exile and Marriage

Lenin was exiled to Siberia in 1897, first visiting his sick mother for a week. Once again, his mother helped him by petitioning the government for all kinds of leniency. Lenin was allowed to travel to Siberia alone, and he was permitted to stay in a more southern Siberian province because of his supposed ill health.[4]

Nadezhda Krupskaya, herself arrested and exiled to Siberia, was granted permission to be transferred to Shushenskoe, where Lenin was, to serve her term. She and Lenin were married in July 1898. Although there appeared to be some genuine affection between the couple, it was Krupskaya's willingness to be a dedicated revolutionary and a devoted follower of Lenin that cemented their relationship right from the beginning.[5]

Being an exile in Siberia at that time meant freedom to pursue revolutionary study and writing. Books and articles arrived by mail, and Lenin grew healthy on a routine of reading, writing, and walking in the clear air. His wife became his valued assistant. She helped him with editing and listened as the chapters of his first major book, *The Development of Capitalism in Russia*, reached completion.[6]

Lenin and his wife, Nadezhda Krupskaya, are seen here in later years with some young relatives.

Problems With the Movement

Meanwhile, the revolutionaries who had not been arrested were experiencing problems. Although they had formed a group called the Russian Social Democratic Labor party (RSDLP), they were continually watched by the police. Once again, because of fear of the police—and even of change itself—the workers did not welcome their ideas. However, the idea of trade unions—instead of revolution—as a means of lessening the workers' plight was gaining ground with the help of liberals.

Lenin felt that if the workers were not organized by revolutionaries, they would simply give in to capitalism and continue to be oppressed. While he was in Siberia, Lenin wrote another book. He borrowed Nikolai Chernyshevski's title *What Is to Be Done?*

Source Document

[T]o concentrate all secret functions in the hands of as small a number of professional revolutionaries as possible does not mean that the latter will "do the thinking for all" and that the crowd will not take an active part in the *movement*. On the contrary, the crowd will advance from its ranks increasing numbers of professional revolutionaries, for it will know that it is not enough for a few students and workingmen, waging economic war, to gather together and form a "committee," but that it takes years to train professional revolutionaries; the crowd will "think" not of primitive ways but of training professional revolutionaries.[7]

Lenin wrote many works outlining his ideas on how a Communist revolution should take place. Among them was his famous What Is to Be Done?

Lenin's book, which would be published in Germany in 1902, solidified Lenin's revolutionary theory that, "unless the workers were led by a socialist party composed of professional revolutionaries, they would betray their class interests (as understood by socialists) and sell out."[8] For Lenin, this meant that the workers simply would never even understand their own interests as a class. They needed to be taught by professionals, like himself and his party. These beliefs would eventually lead to the worst excesses of the Russian Revolution.

Chapter 6

Solidifying Leadership

Immediately after finishing his term of exile in Siberia on February 10, 1900, Lenin went forward with plans to start an underground newspaper. It was to be called *Iskra*, or "the Spark."[1] This paper would literally be carried around Russia by a handful of dedicated revolutionaries, most of whom Lenin had recruited in Siberia.

Iskra would have to be written and printed outside of Russia. While Lenin was in Siberia, there had been wide-scale arrests of the remaining Marxist intellectuals in St. Petersburg. In addition, a document called *Credo of the Young*, by Ekaterina Kuskova, furthered the separation of liberal and social democratic (Marxist) methods of reform. The liberals favored trade unions, for instance, while the Marxists believed that professional revolutionaries should organize the workers to revolt against the government. Kuskova's work urged reformers to follow the path that seemed most suited for Russia: Since the tsar had cut off all political action, Russian workers should form trade unions and strike for economic gain.[2]

This went totally against Lenin's belief in revolution. He worried so much about this attitude during his last months in Siberia that he lost weight and sleep.[3] By the time he left Siberia, he had engineered a meeting with seventeen exiles, and smuggled out a document called "The Protest by the Russian Social Democrats."[4]

Switzerland and *Iskra*

Lenin planned to go to Switzerland to meet once again with Plekhanov, his hero, and begin implementing his plans for *Iskra*. He had no trouble obtaining a visa, but before leaving the country, he visited his wife, who was ill, and his mother in Moscow. He also made more revolutionary contacts in the provinces. He even took the chance of returning to St. Petersburg. With Yuli Martov, Lenin was caught by the police carrying two thousand rubles (Russian currency)—startup money for his newspaper. Miraculously, he was released and the money was not confiscated.

Lenin and another revolutionary named Alexander Potresov left immediately for Switzerland. Once there, things did not go so smoothly.

Lenin had a very forceful personality. He had emerged as the leader of the militant wing of Marxists within Russia. Plekhanov, on the other hand, was the undisputed revolutionary leader in exile. Plekhanov was critical of Lenin's writing style, and it was clear that he had no plan to give up his role as leader of the revolution to Lenin. He intended to be *Iskra*'s major contributor of ideas.[5]

Lenin was disillusioned, but he was not about to give up control of anything. It was at this point that he stopped using pseudonyms—pen names—for his writing. The name V. I. Lenin, which may have come from the name of the River Lena in Siberia, became his fixed public identity.[6]

Although Plekhanov was granted two votes on decisions for the newspaper instead of the one vote each of the other five *Iskra* editors had, Lenin managed to get around this by having the newspaper printed in Germany instead of Switzerland. Plekhanov, in Switzerland, could only vote by mail—and the paper had to get printed on schedule whether Plekhanov's votes arrived or not.

When Nadezhda Krupskaya left Siberia, Lenin made her the secretary of *Iskra*, placing even more control over the paper in his own hands. *Iskra*, printed regularly and smuggled by revolutionaries to groups within Russia who faithfully handed it out, brought Lenin solid recognition as a prominent leader in exile.

Making Money in Exile

How did the growing number of exiled Marxist revolutionaries manage to eat, pay their rent, and finance all their comings and goings in and out of Russia and other European cities? Historian Dmitri Volkogonov pointed out that "At the time of the revolution of 1917, Lenin . . . had spent all of two years in paid work."[7] That had been when Lenin was a lawyer in St. Petersburg. Strangely, the majority of the professional revolutionaries—champions of the working class— had never known what it was like to work for a living. If they had been employed, there would never have been enough time to do all the writing, running back and forth, and agitating that preceded the Russian Revolution.

Lenin earned a small amount of money from the many pamphlets and articles he published in *Iskra* and elsewhere, but he was mainly supported until his mother's death by her pension and the sale of the family estate in Samara. Private benefactors also helped the revolutionary movement, including sympathizers such as famous writer Maxim Gorky and other wealthy Russians. Increasingly, there were also party funds available, some of which came from "expropriations"— just plain stealing. A raid on two carriages filled with banknotes in Tbilisi, Georgia, the country south of Russia, killed three people and wounded many others. The robbery was carried out to obtain party funds. Since the banknotes were in large denominations, however, some of these were still uncashed by 1917, when the revolution began. All over Europe, revolutionaries were arrested when they tried to cash these notes.[8]

Most of the "expropriations," however, were of smaller sizes. Added to the donations from the ten thousand party members who lived in Russia after 1905, funding for revolutionary activity was never at risk. Lenin taught himself to handle money and keep books. He became accountant of all revolutionary funds.

A Split in the Party

Between 1901 and 1905, the Marxist revolutionaries gained strength. But they also suffered a major split in ideologies.

The second congress (meeting) of the RSDLP was held in Brussels, Belgium, starting on July 30, 1903. To avoid police surveillance, it was then reopened in London on August 11 of that year. Although the congress was meant to help unite the revolutionaries, the result was instead a split into two different factions— the Bolsheviks and the Mensheviks.

Lenin headed the Bolsheviks, while the group headed mainly by Martov was called the Mensheviks. Though *Bolshevik* means "majority-ite," or the majority group, and *Menshevik* means "minority-ite," or minority group, the Mensheviks were actually in the majority at the second party congress.

The Mensheviks were the more moderate wing of the party. They believed that violence as a weapon for social change could be avoided through democracy, a parliament (legislature), and more than one political party. Their ultimate goal was democracy.

The Bolsheviks, on the other hand, while still giving lip service in some of their writings to democracy, used it as no more than a political show. Lenin and his followers believed in the value of violence. They equated social democracy with reform and Marxism with power. The dictatorship of the proletariat—carried out by a small, elite group of professional revolutionaries who hoped for world revolution—justified any means needed to bring it about. The Bolsheviks envisioned a nationless, classless world, with Russia as only one part.

Party Rivalry

These differences among the revolutionary factions were covered up by endless talk about organization. Who should join the party? What level of dedication—particularly to violent overthrow—was mandatory? Should there be a special combat organization?

When the third party congress was held in London in the spring of 1905, Lenin would give an impassioned speech about the need for armed violence. He tried to convince the congress that revolution was just around the corner. In his view, it was the Mensheviks, with their desire for peaceful change, who were getting in the way. Conciliation with any reform movement, including the Mensheviks, was against the Marxist cause and must be stopped. Meanwhile, back in Russia, where economic and social deprivation continued, more people were growing ready to heed Lenin's call to arms.

Chapter 7

Bloody Sunday and Its Aftermath

While Lenin and his professional revolutionaries were arguing and agitating by means of pamphlets smuggled into Russia, all social classes in that country were objecting to the continued oppression of the tsarist system. Workers, peasants, and professionals were coming together and striking to demand representative government.

War With Japan

In 1904, Russia went to war against Japan. At issue was control over Chinese territory in Manchuria. This war, waged six thousand miles from the Russian capital of St. Petersburg, meant that soldiers had to be mobilized and huge expenses had to be devoted to buying arms and supplying the troops.

It is important to understand the background behind this ill-advised war. Sergei Witte, a skilled diplomat who had been an advisor to two tsars, urged Tsar Alexander III to create funds to build a railway across Siberia. This Trans-Siberian Railway, 5,876 miles long, was begun in 1891 and would be completed in 1916. As work neared completion on the final eastern segment, the Russians asked China for permission to run tracks through Chinese Manchuria to shorten the trip from Lake Baikal in southeastern Russia to the port at Vladivostok on the Pacific coast. China granted permission, but made it clear that the only Russian presence in Mongolia should be the railroad and its employees.[1]

By the time these negotiations took place with China, Nicholas II had become tsar. Under his leadership, Russia immediately broke its agreement and introduced police and military units to Mongolia. In fact, Russia made plans to annex—take over as its own territory—Chinese Manchuria. Problems arose because Japan, too, wished to take over the area.

Tsar Nicholas II proved to be an ineffective leader whose policies would help lead to the Russian Revolution.

In February 1904, with no warning, Japan attacked a naval base Russia had leased from the Chinese at Port Arthur in Manchuria. The Japanese laid siege to the base, sank a great many ships, and took control of the China Sea. At first, the Russian people rallied to help the war effort. As the war dragged on, however, opinion changed dramatically.

Social Unrest

Because the war was going on thousands of miles away from St. Petersburg, troops made up of peasants and workers had to travel a great distance at great expense to fight the Japanese. Political unrest grew in opposition to the war—and the government. The hated minister of the interior, Vyacheslav Plehve, a master at police espionage, was assassinated. As it became apparent that Russia was losing the war, social democratic and liberal groups went into action to demonstrate their opposition to the government and the war. In December 1904, the Russians at Port Arthur surrendered. The Japanese captured whatever they had not already destroyed of Russia's Pacific fleet and took twenty-five thousand prisoners.

Father Gapon and the Workers' March

For several years before the war, a priest named Father Georgi Gapon had been busy establishing trade unions in St. Petersburg. At first, he had been persuaded to do this by the police, who thought unions they helped set up would avoid strikes and control the activities of the labor movement. Over time, however,

Father Gapon came to identify with the grievances of the workers, and began to take their side in conflicts with government authorities—who had hired him in the first place.[2]

In January 1905, thousands of workers who had been dismissed from a large industrial plant held a protest march. Although most workers were still loyal to the tsar, they did want to gain more representation for their needs in the government. Father Gapon helped the workers organize a peaceful demonstration. He received permission from the police to hold the march, as long as the protesters did not get too close to the Winter Palace, one of the tsar's homes. Gapon did not know that Nicholas, to whom the workers were appealing for fair treatment, had left St. Petersburg the night before.

On Sunday morning, January 22, a quiet procession of workers holding religious symbols called icons carried a petition to their tsar. As the procession got close to the palace, armed troops met it and told its members to leave. When the marchers did not obey immediately, the panicked troops fired on the crowd, killing two hundred people and wounding eight hundred others.[3]

Shock and outrage in response to the incident—called "Bloody Sunday"—reached all over the world.[4] Now all organizations—liberal and moderate, social democrats and socialist revolutionaries—protested the violence and condemned the government. Although there had been a history of workers' strikes in Russia since the 1870s, the Bloody Sunday demonstration marked the first time workers so forcefully appealed to the government for dramatic changes. After the bloodshed, hundreds of thousands of other workers went on strike, blaming the government for the outrageously violent incident.

The Tsar's Response

Tsar Nicholas II, an often indecisive leader, took some measures to try to get the situation back under control. One of these measures was to declare the universities exempt from police surveillance and interference. All this did was open up the universities for the many radical groups, which were beginning to feel left out of the mass protests, and allow them to continue to agitate. Liberals, meanwhile, founded a group they called the Union of Unions. Many professional associations joined. It called for a constitutional monarchy to replace the tsar's autocracy.

By May 1905, Japan had completed the humiliation of Russia by sinking the Russian ships that had tried to come to the rescue of the fleet the Japanese had already sunk earlier in the war. United States President Theodore Roosevelt stepped in and offered to act as an intermediary between Russia and Japan. Diplomat Sergei Witte went to meet with Japanese representatives in Portsmouth, New Hampshire, in the United States.

Witte was able to negotiate terms that were far better than Russia could have expected. Russia was able to keep far eastern lands of the empire, with the exception of the Liaodong peninsula, the South Manchurian Railway, and the southern half of Sakhalin Island. Despite having been humiliated terribly in the war, Russia would remain a powerful nation on the Pacific, to the dismay of Japan. Although he was pleased with the good peace terms he had won, Witte returned home to a Russian Empire that was in disarray.

A Brewing Revolution

A national strike of essential services, including the railroad that was needed to bring Russian troops home from the east, was called. In October, the Union of Unions got strike committees ready to bring the country literally to a halt.

Tsar Nicholas called in Sergei Witte, who told the tsar there were two options: Nicholas could either declare the country a military dictatorship, or he could grant major political concessions to the disgruntled people. Witte knew that the first option was impossible. The army was six thousand miles away, and the railroads were not running. However, he knew he had to offer that option to Nicholas because it was the option the tsar would have preferred to implement, if it had been practical.[5] The other option—granting major changes—was the only real choice. Witte believed that if Nicholas could take charge of reforms and create a constitution, the appeal of the revolutionary factions would weaken. Witte stated in a prophetic memorandum:

> The advance of human progress is unstoppable. The idea of human freedom will triumph, if not by way of reform, then by way of revolution. But in the latter event it will come to life on the ashes of a thousand years of destroyed history. The Russian rebellion, mindless and pitiless, will sweep away everything, turn everything to dust. What kind of Russia will emerge from this unexampled trial transcends human imagination: the horrors of the Russian rebellion may surpass everything known to history. . . . Attempts to put into practice the ideals of theoretical socialism— they will fail but they will be made, no doubt about it—will destroy the family, the expressions of religious faith, property, all the foundations of law.[6]

Despite Witte's warning, Nicholas did not act. He held conferences with everyone he thought might be able to give him advice. His cousin Grand Duke Nikolai Nikolaevich told him that a military dictatorship was impossible. He also said that if Nicholas did not grant political liberties to Russia, he would shoot himself.[7]

The October Manifesto

Once again, Witte stepped in. He drafted a manifesto (statement) that guaranteed civil rights for the Russian people and an elected legislature to be called the Duma. Finally, on October 30, Tsar Nicholas II, making sure the document did not contain the word *constitution*, signed the October Manifesto.

Source Document

The disturbances and unrest in St Petersburg, Moscow and in many other parts of our Empire . . . could give rise to national instability and present a threat to the unity of Our State. The oath which We took as Tsar compels Us to use all Our strength, intelligence and power to put a speedy end to this unrest which is so dangerous for the State. . . . [I]n view of the need to speedily implement earlier measures to pacify the country, we have decided that the work of the government must be unified. We have therefore ordered the government to take the following measures . . . :

1. Fundamental civil freedoms will be granted to the population, including real personal inviolability, freedom of conscience, speech, assembly and association.

2. Participation in the Duma will be granted to those classes of the population which are at present deprived of voting powers. . . .

3. It is established as an unshakeable rule that no law can come into force without its approval by the State Duma and representatives of the people will be given the opportunity to take real part in the supervision of the legality of government bodies.

We call on all true sons of Russia to remember the homeland, to help put a stop to this unprecedented unrest and, together with this, to devote all their strength to the restoration of peace to their native land.[8]

After the 1905 revolution, Tsar Nicholas II issued a manifesto granting the people of Russia many new civil rights.

The signing of the October Manifesto effectively ended autocracy in Russia—but it did not solve Russia's problems. In fact, in the months after these political changes, excesses of all kinds occurred. Conservative Russians, who were loyal to the tsar and did not want to see the autocracy end, carried out pogroms—killing sprees that often wiped out whole villages—against Jews, simply because many social revolutionaries were Jewish. The peasants, confused by this mayhem, decided that they had license to seize private property from landowners. No one stepped in to stop this chaos. The new legislative process had not yet been implemented, and Tsar Nicholas was in no hurry to do anything about it.

The tsar was acting as if the revolution had never occurred. This attitude made the Duma, even after it began sessions, ineffective. Conservatives became more conservative and radical revolutionaries more radical during the first ten years in which the new political institutions were supposed to be in place.

Chapter 8

The Bolsheviks and Mensheviks

The events leading up to and including the October Manifesto were not lost on Russian revolutionaries. The Bolsheviks organized to send agents to Russian prisoners of war in Chinese Manchuria to pass out Marxist revolutionary literature. The Mensheviks within Russia tried to come up with practical solutions to the political crisis, but made no headway.[1]

The only cooperation that occurred between the many small revolutionary factions took place during the pre-Manifesto period. Each crisis that arose was used as an opportunity to keep Russian workers thinking in a revolutionary way.[2]

Chief among those who made use of social unrest to promote revolution was a group called the St. Petersburg Soviet of Workers' Deputies. Through this group, Leon Trotsky, a social democrat who refused to

This poster celebrates the 1905 revolution in Russia that paved the way for a complete overthrow of the tsarist system.

ally himself with either Bolshevik or Menshevik factions, came to fame as a revolutionary. Trotsky was an excellent speaker who had strong appeal to large numbers of people.[3]

Shortly after the October Manifesto was signed, Trotsky was arrested and condemned to lifelong exile in the farthest reaches of Siberia. Just before reaching his final destination, he escaped. Wearing two fur coats and two pairs of boots, Trotsky made his way back across the snows of Siberia. Trotsky ended up in Finland. He attempted to be a conciliator between the Bolshevik and Menshevik factions.[4] The Mensheviks believed in pushing for action that would arise spontaneously from a large power base, including the masses of Russian people. The Bolsheviks, under Lenin's leadership, believed that a mass movement could only

be brought about and controlled by a small, chosen, dedicated elite of professional revolutionaries.[5]

Third Party Congress

In exile, the RSDLP continued to feud within itself along organizational and ideological lines. Lenin decided to leave *Iskra* and start an entirely new Bolshevik paper, which he called *Vpered* (Forward). *Iskra*, now under the more egalitarian leadership of Yuli Martov, a Menshevik and Lenin's former close colleague, became a forum for debate. It was no longer the beacon of revolutionary leadership Lenin had hoped it would be.

The RSDLP called a third party congress. It was held in London in April 1905. This congress was supposed to work toward reconciliation between Bolsheviks and Mensheviks. Instead, it became a Bolshevik congress when most Mensheviks, led by Plekhanov and Martov, refused to attend. This left Lenin poised to be the dominant leader of his party.[6] During the congress, he worked to organize his fellow Bolsheviks and to make the party ready for revolution— when the opportunity arrived.

The Bolsheviks and the October Manifesto

Lenin left for St. Petersburg shortly after the October Manifesto was issued. He arrived in November 1905. The country was in turmoil. All reformist organizations were both reveling in changes and pushing for

Source Document

In calling the strike, all the revolutionary parties, all the Moscow unions recognised and even intuitively felt that it must inevitably grow into an uprising. . . . From a strike and demonstrations to isolated barricades. From isolated barricades to the mass erection of barricades and street fighting against the troops. Over the heads of the organisations, the mass proletarian struggle developed from a strike to an uprising. This is the greatest historic gain the Russian revolution achieved in . . . 1905; and like all preceding gains it was purchased at the price of enormous sacrifices. The movement was raised from a general political strike to a higher stage. It compelled the reaction *to go to the limit* in its resistance, and so brought vastly nearer the moment when the revolution will also go to the limit in applying the means of attack. The reaction *cannot* go further than the shelling of barricades, buildings and crowds. But the revolution can go very much further than the Moscow volunteer fighting units, it can go very, very much further in breadth and depth. And the revolution has advanced far since December. The base of the revolutionary crisis has become immeasurably broader—the blade must now be sharpened to a keener edge. . . . As is always the case, practice marched ahead of theory, A peaceful strike and demonstrations immediately ceased to satisfy the workers; they asked: What is to be done next?[7]

Lenin discussed the 1905 revolution and what it meant for his dream of a future revolution in "Lessons of the Moscow Uprising."

more change with a united voice. Lenin, however, considered himself a leader. He would not join a faction to work from within. He contented himself with spreading the goal of eventual revolution, living in disguise and moving frequently to escape the police.

Over the next months, however, he softened his position. Lenin encouraged Bolsheviks to try to take part in the government, starting with the Duma elections. He argued that this new legislature would be a perfect place to spread information about the RSDLP. He even advocated a reunion with the Mensheviks.[8]

Despite these views, the period after the October Manifesto—between 1907 and the outbreak of World War I in 1914—saw increasing conflict between the two branches of the party, despite a fourth party congress in 1906. Over time, Lenin's views would again become radical, but for the moment, he wanted to increase the party's strength in any way possible.

Party membership, which was at its peak at the time of the fifth party congress in the spring of 1907, began to dwindle. After the congress, Lenin did not return to Russia, for fear of capture. It would be almost ten years before he returned.

Continued Exile

It looked as if Lenin's power, along with his exile, might continue without his ever seeing the revolution. Although terrorist activity still went on in Russia, it, too, dwindled as the government became stronger. With each year's new Duma elections, there were fewer socialists and liberals and more conservative and propertied members, which pleased the tsar. Even those revolutionary members who did remain seemed to be part of a shaky institution. In both 1906 and 1907, Tsar Nicholas II dismissed the Duma when he deemed it too radical. Not until the third Duma, beginning in November 1907, did the legislature serve a full term without the tsar's interference.

Sergei Witte managed to bring in foreign loans and draft a constitution for Russia. He began to implement the civil liberties promised by the October Manifesto, but then was himself suspected by the government of gaining too much power. He was dismissed. The tsar and his advisors further limited the powers of the Duma and the liberties granted by the October Manifesto. Then Petr A. Stolypin, Minister of the Interior, came on the scene.

Stolypin Takes Charge

Pëtr A. Stolypin was an even more skilled politician than Witte. He acted quickly to suppress acts of terrorism, executing those people suspected of rebellion. He also worked to secure foreign loans and to take steps toward agrarian—land use—reform. He presented the Duma with a law that allowed peasant families to withdraw from the communes, the social and land use system the government had decreed for the peasants, and apply for ownership of the land they had been allotted. This measure was not totally popular. The peasants had grown used to the security offered by communal land. By 1917, only 10 percent of eligible peasant households had chosen to become independent of the commune.

Wealthy landowners did not like this new law, either. They wanted to be the dominant force in rural Russia. Stolypin ran into problems from all factions as he tried to introduce bills that would actually make the Duma a partner in governing Russia. The tsar's government rebuffed his efforts because it had not wanted to end the autocracy in the first place. Liberals and socialists, on the other hand, worried that Stolypin's reforms would be successful, and that the revolution would be diluted and eventually buried.

An assassin's bullet ended Stolypin's life in 1911. While the next three years seemed relatively peaceful in Russia, anxiety lay just beneath the surface. There was still no agreement among conflicting political factions. Hatred between ethnic groups and social classes was held in uneasy check only by the presence of the army and police. This delicate balance would not last long. Russia would soon be at war once again—both from within and from without.

World War I

For Lenin, the years after the October Manifesto were frustrating. For the only time in their lives, he and his wife were living in near poverty. They moved frequently throughout Europe, but still could not return to Russia, and Lenin's renewed radical stance—demanding revolution or nothing—had alienated him from all Mensheviks and even many of the Bolsheviks.

Two loyal followers stayed with him. Grigori Zinoviev and Lev Kamenev started a new revolutionary newspaper. It would become Lenin's main vehicle for furthering the Bolshevik cause. *Zvezda* (*The Star*), as the paper was called, was distributed secretly in St. Petersburg.

In April 1912, Russian government troops killed hundreds of striking mine workers, causing more

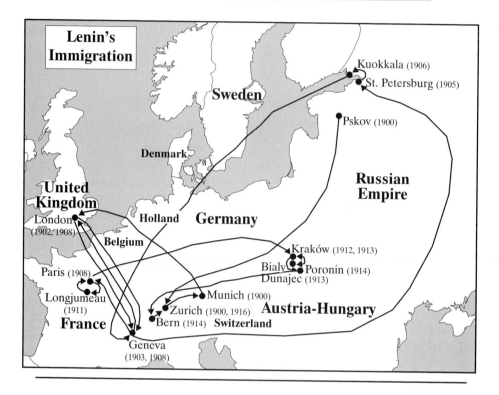

As an exile, Lenin moved around throughout Europe. This map shows some of the places he called home during the many years he was not allowed to return to Russia.

strikes and violent reaction. The RSDLP was able to organize a legal worker newspaper, called *Pravda* (*Truth*), using Bolshevik funds. The paper, based in St. Petersburg, was very successful, but it only got Lenin into more trouble with the Mensheviks because it so clearly put forth his Bolshevik ideas.

Nicholas, Alexandra, and Rasputin

Tsar Nicholas II made many mistakes during the years before the Russian Revolution. An indecisive man, he could not see beyond the traditional autocracy Russia had had for centuries. Forced by circumstances to sign the October Manifesto in 1905, he and his regime did their best to undermine any real liberty being offered to the Russian people. And yet, because of the customary adoration the peasant masses had for the role of the tsar, the end of the autocracy was not welcomed by the majority of the people it was meant to help.

Not only was Nicholas indecisive, but he was married to a woman who always urged him to make decisions in terms of autocracy. Empress Alexandra, who had been born a wealthy German princess and a granddaughter of England's Queen Victoria, came under the influence of a mystic named Rasputin. A monk with astounding powers of persuasion, Rasputin was able to cast hypnotic spells that helped Alexis, the tsar's son, who was a hemophiliac—someone whose blood does not clot normally and bleeds excessively when injured. The young prince seemed to benefit from Rasputin's treatments for his painful and life-threatening disease. Empress Alexandra was so grateful for Rasputin's help in easing her son's suffering that he became her advisor in all matters, even politics, though she chose to take his advice only when it suited her. Rasputin advised the tsar and his wife against entering World War I.[1]

The Beginning of War

World War I broke out in 1914 after Archduke Franz Ferdinand of Austria-Hungary was assassinated by a

Serbian nationalist. The nations of Europe quickly took sides: Germany and Austria-Hungary formed the Central Powers with their allies, while Serbia, Great Britain, France, Russia, and other nations formed the Allied Powers.

Of all the mistakes Nicholas II made, becoming involved in World War I was perhaps his worst. At first, the war brought out national loyalties, inspiring some cooperation among the various factions and classes, and drawing attention away from internal unrest. Spirits were high when Russia mounted a successful offensive in Prussia (a German state, now part of Russia, Lithuania, Poland, and Germany) against Germany, and in Carpathia (located in the region of the Carpathian Mountains on the border between Belorussia and Poland) against Austrian-Hungarian troops. But this enthusiasm for the war did not last for long.

In the fall of 1914, at the Battle of Tannenberg in Germany, an attacking Russian army was left without backup forces. Two entire Russian corps, trapped in the woods, surrendered. Then, in the Battle of Masurian Lakes, a retreating German army routed the Russians, who lost one hundred twenty thousand men. By the time the two battles were over, the Russian Army had lost two hundred fifty thousand men—a quarter of its troops. Because of poorly maintained railroads, the rest of the Russian Army in Germany ran out of weapons and then out of food. The Russian Army was starving to death and vulnerable to attack.

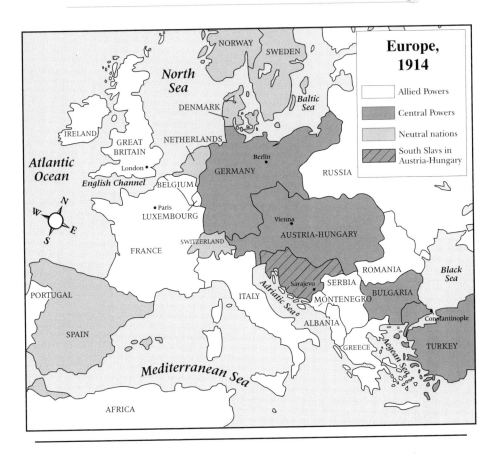

Europe, 1914

- Allied Powers
- Central Powers
- Neutral nations
- South Slavs in Austria-Hungary

This map shows how the nations of Europe were divided into alliances during World War I.

The soldiers lived in chaos, lashing out at each other and their superiors.

On the advice of his wife and Rasputin, Tsar Nicholas decided to fire the head Russian Army commander, his uncle the Grand Duke Nikolai Nikolaevich. Nicholas himself would become Commander in Chief of the armed forces. He would devote himself full-time to fighting the war. Although his presence stabilized the worst of the anarchy in the army, Nicholas left Russia to be run by Empress Alexandra and Rasputin. During his absence, strikes happened regularly, food became scarce to the point of famine, and inflation and corruption were everywhere. Still, the tsar refused to step in and change decisions that were made by his wife.

Finally, the entire country seemed to have had enough of this ineffective tsar. In late 1916, angry members of the nobility assassinated Rasputin, hoping the government would be better without his influence. Even that move, however, came too late. "The regime proved incapable of governing in a critical situation," according to historian Dmitri Volkogonov.[2] A major revolution was about to occur—but where were its leaders?

Revolutionary Leaders and the War

Socialists from all of the countries participating in World War I were divided into three camps: Defensists basically felt they should shelve revolutionary activity and help their native country fight the war. Internationalists disagreed, believing that workers—no matter what country they came from—should not be killing each other to make the capitalist system stronger. Defeatists hoped their own country would lose the war, because they believed a defeat would weaken the government that the socialists were working to destroy.

Lenin believed in both of the latter two positions. He saw the war as an excellent opportunity to further the Marxist revolution. Because he was living in Austrian Poland at the time, which was at war with Russia, he was arrested in the early days of the war by the Austrian police. However, he was able to convince the authorities that he wanted nothing to do with Russia's war effort. He was allowed to move to Switzerland with his wife.

There, he went to the libraries, took long walks, and continued his writing. Lenin's financial conditions grew worse, partly because of the death of his mother, who had helped support him through all the years of his exile.

Because of the war, communications to and from Russia were difficult. The Germans, however, saw in Lenin a chance to further their own efforts. In conversations with Lenin, German officials took in the major messages of his revolutionary writing. It was the Germans, not the Bolsheviks, who flooded the Russian war trenches with revolutionary propaganda.

Despite the unrest in Russia, the army's terrible situation, and the shift in public mood about the tsar, only parts of this nationwide despair filtered out of Russia to the isolated exiles. In early 1917, the forty-seven-year-old Lenin gave a speech celebrating the 1905 revolution, which he had hoped would be a prelude to a future Marxist revolution. He recognized, however, that this second revolution seemed to be a long way off. To a small audience, he said, "We old folks may not live to see the decisive battles of the coming revolution."[3] He was wrong.

Chapter 10

The Fall
of the Tsar

The war dragged on into 1917. Wood was scarce and bread was scarcer during one of the worst Russian winters on record. Snow had cut off what was left of the railroad lines. Factories were forced to close because of fuel shortages. As the weather turned warmer in late February, more than sixty thousand hungry workers were lining up in front of bakeries for bread to feed their families. For the first time, many troops, including the tsar's own soldiers, did not fire on demonstrators. Even they were disgusted with the war and with the tsarist government.

On March 8, crowds milled about on the main avenue of Petrograd. The Russian capital had been renamed at the start of the war because Russians believed "St. Petersburg" sounded too German. People held up signs saying, "Down with the

Autocracy" and "Down with the War."[1] Those who stood in the breadlines soon broke up and joined the rioting crowd. Looting began. City services soon came to a halt.

Mass Disruption

The tsar's ministers realized that something drastic had to be done. There had never been such mass disruption in Russia. They sent word to the tsar, who was in far-off Mogilev in the south of Russia, monitoring the war effort and caring for his children, who had measles. As usual, Nicholas II underestimated the problems and what had to be done to solve them. He sent word to Petrograd that force must be used to stop the rioting. Within a few days, enough troops had been gathered to make the city appear calm.

On March 10, however, a regiment of soldiers fired on a group of protesters when they refused to leave. Forty civilians were killed or wounded. This incident, in turn, caused a mutiny in a garrison that was composed of men who had been recruited past the usual draft age because all the young men were already at the war front. These men—one hundred sixty thousand of them who were cooped up in barracks that usually accommodated twenty thousand—were in no mood to shoot their fellow Russians in order to defend a government they now hated. The men refused to obey future orders to shoot at civilians, and many other regiments followed suit.

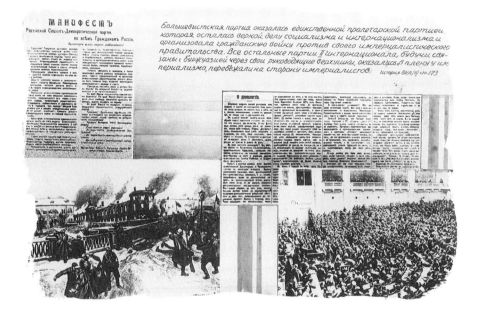

This composite photo depicts some of the major events in the history of the Russian Revolution.

On March 11, a crowd invaded the city's Litovski Prison and burned it down.[2] Rioters also raided the Ministry of the Interior, stole weapons from military arsenals, and hung a red flag (red was a Communist symbol) over the tsar's Winter Palace. The few remaining loyal troops shot rioters and demonstrators, but Petrograd was clearly being run by peasants, who were, by now, in uniform.

The Duma Rallies

The Duma, ignoring Nicholas's recent orders to dissolve, met. Its members had no idea what to do, but it realized it was the only alternative to the tsar and that it had to do something.[3] Thousands of people—soldiers, peasants, and workers—were marching to Taurida Palace where the Duma met, proclaiming allegiance to a body of legislators that was itself confused and divided politically.

On March 12, the Duma rallied, however, and agreed to establish a new government and a whole new social order for Russia. It would form a Provisional Government, to be headed by M. Radzianko, the Duma chairman. This was done in the absence of any revolutionary leaders, who on the same day formed the Petrograd Soviet (a representative governmental body that would rival the Duma for power). This act was initiated mainly by the Mensheviks. The Soviet represented workers and soldiers. Out of three thousand deputies, "more than 2000 were soldiers—this in a city that had two or three times as many industrial workers as servicemen. These figures illustrate the extent to which the February Revolution in its initial phase was a soldier mutiny."[4]

There were many people in the Soviet, all of whom had the right to make long speeches. This meant that no decisions would be made at the first meetings of the Petrograd Soviet. An executive committee was formed, the *Ispolkom*. It acted to unify and organize socialist groups, under the name of the full Soviet. Unlike the Duma, the Ispolkom worked to further, rather than end, the revolution.[5]

The Provisional Government

Although the Provisional Government held the official leadership role between March and November 1917, the government was in fact run by the Ispolkom. By immediately dissolving the police and calling for nationwide elections for self-government, the Ispolkom canceled all provincial bureaucracy—offices that ran the countryside: "They abolished in one fell swoop the entire administrative and security structure that had kept the Russian state intact for a century or more," wrote historian Richard Pipes.[6] Another disastrous mistake was that the government was given no real authority over the armed and angry peasant soldiers.

The most important leader to emerge from this chaos was Alexander Kerensky, a thirty-six-year-old lawyer. He was, interestingly, the son of the Alexander Kerensky who, as a school director, had recommended young Vladimir Lenin for college. The younger

Kerensky was an excellent, emotional speaker, energetic and vain. He had risen to political power by representing striking gold miners in 1905. He was a moderate socialist, a believer in labor causes who was able to win the loyalty of workers, soldiers, moderate socialists, and even some of the radical socialists. He proclaimed from balconies that Russia's suffering was over, and that there would soon be world peace. He was the one leader who was a member of both the Provisional Government and the Ispolkom—for which Lenin would never forgive him.

The Tsar Abdicates

Tsar Nicholas II, who still could not believe that he had actually lost power, was approaching Petrograd in his train as the city fell to the new Provisional Government. On the train, he considered proclaiming Russia a constitutional monarchy. These thoughts, however, came years too late. Perhaps, had Nicholas been able to make peace quickly with Germany and bring back the troops to help regain the city, the revolution might have been contained. Though he considered this, Nicholas became convinced that for the good of Russia, he would have to abdicate—give up his position as tsar of Russia.

Nicholas was met at his train by two members of the Provisional Government. They demanded that he step down from the throne. Nicholas abdicated, not in favor of his son, Alexis, whose hemophilia might cause his death before he reached adulthood, but instead

Source Document

By the Grace of God, We, Nikolai II, Emperor of All the Russias, Tsar of Poland, Grand Duke of Finland, and so forth, to all our faithful subjects be it known:

. . . In these decisive days in the life of Russia we have thought that we owed to our people the close union and organisation of all its forces for the realisation of a rapid victory; for which reason, in agreement with the Imperial Duma, we have recognized that it is for the good of the country that we should abdicate the Crown of the Russian State and lay down the Supreme Power.

Not wishing to separate ourselves from our beloved son, we bequeath our heritage to our brother, the Grand Duke Mikhail Alexandrovich, with our blessing for the future of the Throne of the Russian State. . . .

We call upon all faithful sons of our native land to fulfil their sacred and patriotic duty of obeying the Tsar at the painful moment of national trial and to aid them, together with the representatives of the nation, to conduct the Russian State in the way of prosperity and glory.

May God help Russia.[7]

Tsar Nicholas II issued this address, telling the Russian people of his decision to give up the throne in favor of his brother.

Nicholas's younger brother Michael. Grand Duke Michael, angered by this unwanted "privilege" and afraid for his life, refused to accept the throne. With his refusal, the Russian monarchy was dissolved.

Nicholas and his family were placed under house arrest at Tsarskoe Selo, one of their country homes near Petrograd. There, they would remain for five months while the Provisional Government tried to decide what should be done with them.

The Exiles Return

Exiles from Siberia and from countries all over the world now began their trips home to Russia. One of the first to arrive was Joseph Stalin, who came originally from the southern Russian province of Georgia. Stalin was an active Bolshevik who had been an editor of *Pravda* before he was arrested and sent to Siberia. He and Lev Kamenev found themselves the most influential Bolsheviks present in Petrograd in March. They decided to explore compromise with the Provisional Government, so as to appear to be in tune with the mood of the masses.[8] Stalin also spoke of trying to find common ground with the Mensheviks and other revolutionary groups.

Leon Trotsky, who had been running a socialist newspaper in Brooklyn, New York, did not arrive in Petrograd until May. Though he was of great use to the party because of his intelligence and his incisive, charismatic, and inflammatory speeches, Trotsky had never been part of the main organizing body of

Joseph Stalin (seen here at right, with Lenin at left) was one of the first Bolsheviks to return to Russia after the start of the revolution.

Bolsheviks. Like Provisional Government leader Alexander Kerensky, Trotsky often allowed personal vanity to interfere with expressing his ideas to other people.

Lenin, on the other hand, had a firmness of purpose that did not waver. Even when his stance made him unpopular, he never appeared personally arrogant. However, Lenin had not yet reached Russia, and there was nothing he could do from afar to bring about compromise among the Bolsheviks. When he reached Russia on April 16, the revolution would take on a different face.

Chapter 11

The Return of Lenin

The train pulled into the Finland station at 11:00 P.M. on April 16. Lenin had notified Pravda to say that he would be arriving not as just another returning exile but as a leader.[1] April 16 was the last day of an All-Russian Bolshevik Conference that was going on in Petrograd. It was also Easter Monday, and all the factories were closed. Preparations for the conference had been elaborate and there was a large crowd gathered. Banners flew, and revolutionary slogans were being uttered. A band played the French national anthem, the "Marseillaise," and an armored car stood ready. Lenin was carried on the shoulders of workers to stand on top of a car and deliver a speech.

In his speech, welcomed by many but shocking to others, Lenin declared his intent not to work with the Provisional Government.[2] He said it had done nothing

Lenin waves to a crowd of supporters from a train platform on his return from exile.

but deceive the people. Lenin promised to continue, with the people, to fight for world revolution.

Lenin was taken to Bolshevik headquarters, a lavish villa the party had taken over from a famous ballerina named M. F. Kshesinskaia, said in her youth to have been the tsar's mistress. At this time, although the Provisional Government was indecisive and the Petrograd Soviet still disorganized, the Bolsheviks had no more than two hundred thousand members and followers. The Russian population at that time was around 150 million. The outer reaches of the empire were only now, as the snows melted, beginning to hear that a revolution had occurred.

The "April Theses"

The very next day, Lenin proposed the so-called "April Theses." This document "impressed most members of his audience as written by someone out of touch with reality, if not positively mad [insane]."[3] At first, *Pravda* refused to print the theses. When it did, the editors wrote an article saying that the theses were only Lenin's views, not their own. "They [the Bolsheviks] were being told by their leader to turn the Soviet into a battering ram, and with it to demolish the Provisional Government," according to historian Harold Shukman.[4]

Lenin's "Theses" called for World War I to stop at any cost, and for the revolution to continue to its next phase—there should be no stopping to allow the middle class to create a democracy. It was time, he said, to move directly to a Marxist, or Communist, state. He said the Provisional Government must be replaced, and a people's militia would replace the army. All land was to be seized in the name of the nation. All power must rest in the Soviets—the popular councils—including all industrial production and distribution. There would be a single national bank. He promised the people peace, bread, and land—welcome words to people who had only recently been on the verge of starvation. Over the next six months, the Bolsheviks' amazing rise to power would make it clear that the "Bolsheviks were bound together not by what they believed but in whom they believed [Lenin]."[5]

Lenin had no intention of merely taking over the existing government bodies. Instead, he would try to eliminate the old institutions entirely, replacing them with new government structures. Lenin would also avoid counterrevolutionary tactics (actions by those who wanted to stop the revolution) by eliminating the counterrevolutionaries—by whatever means necessary.

German Opinion

Germany was delighted that Lenin had taken a hard line on the war. Revolution and a world war were incompatible, and the Germans would be the ones to benefit most from Lenin's ardent antiwar stance. It is clear that German money helped, if not ensured, the Bolsheviks' rise to power. Some estimates put the total amount given by Germany to the Bolsheviks at somewhere between $6 million and $10 million, although this was kept highly secret after Lenin's return.

The Bolsheviks Continue to Agitate

After Lenin published the "April Theses," the next important Bolshevik move was the formation, in May, of the Bolshevik Red Guard, a militia that would grow larger over time. The Bolsheviks were good at organizing. When disagreements between the Provisional Government and the Soviet over ways to handle the war effort led to street demonstrations, the Bolsheviks were right there, spreading antigovernment slogans. They called for the Soviet to take over the government. Despite these forceful tactics on the part of the Bolsheviks, General Lavr Kornilov was turned down by the Provisional Government when he asked to use force against the Bolshevik demonstrators.

This crowd gathered for a May Day celebration in 1917, just a few months after the start of the revolution.

The Provisional Government admitted that it was having little success in running the country. It offered the Bolsheviks positions in the cabinet (executive advisors), an offer they had formerly refused but now decided to accept. Next, the creation of a new coalition government played right into the hands of the Bolsheviks. Dual power—shared by the Provisional Government and the Soviets—had been troublesome. Now the Soviets would dominate the Provisional Government, yet remain an independent body.

As part of the government, however, the Soviets were blamed when things went wrong. Still, the Bolsheviks declared that they were the only alternative—the Soviets alone could save Russia. Since the Bolsheviks wanted world revolution, and did not necessarily feel loyal to Russia itself, historian Richard Pipes explained, "they could . . . act with complete irresponsibility, promising every group whatever it wanted and encouraging every destructive trend."[6]

Antiwar propaganda was carried out quietly among the troops at the war front. Alexander Kerensky, now war minister, gave ringing speeches that rallied troops for hours after he left. But the soldiers were tired after three years—tired of suffering and tired of the mixed attitudes toward the war that were reaching them from Petrograd.

A Failed Coup

In June, the Bolsheviks planned a mass demonstration against the war, but they lacked the centrality of purpose to actually carry it out. The Russian Army had one more victory against Germany, led by General Kornilov, but was then quickly routed by Austrians coming to Germany's aid. For Russia, the war just fell apart. Russians soldiers fled for home.

Once again, the antiwar Bolsheviks organized street riots. Meanwhile, Lenin was in Finland, taking a break. He had been suffering from headaches and, according to a friend, "his face was white and his eyes showed great fatigue."[7] His rest was cut short by the increasing anger at the continuation of the war. Workers and soldiers who did not want to go to the front presented a perfect opportunity for organization by the Bolsheviks. Lenin hurriedly returned to Petrograd.

Though Lenin later claimed that the demonstration he organized on July 17 was meant to be a peaceful means of taking power, it appears that he hoped the time for decisive action had finally come. However, since Lenin had come back to Russia only that morning, news of rioting, looting, pogroms, and general chaos made him lose "his nerve."[8] Perhaps there had not been enough organizing beforehand. Or perhaps, as historian Dmitri Volkogonov believed, "Having brought out half a million people, the Bolsheviks had acted without a clear plan or precise direction."[9] Whatever the reason, Lenin called off the planned coup (government overthrow).

The Provisional Government, frightened because it knew the armed Bolshevik troops could easily have taken over Taurida Palace, where it had its offices, released some information condemning the Bolsheviks for treason in dealings with the Germans. These accusations rallied government troops, who occupied the city, hunting for and arresting Bolsheviks the entire next week. Lenin, a master of disguises, first hid in various safe houses in Petrograd, and then, once again, fled as an exile to Finland.

Chapter 12

The October Coup

By September 1917, the Bolshevik position began to strengthen. The Bolsheviks were helped by Leon Trotsky, whose excellent speaking skills gradually convinced some Russians that the attempted coups were really the fault of the Soviets. But the real favor to the Bolsheviks came through General Kornilov, back from defeat at the war front and angry. Alexander Kerensky had appointed Kornilov Commander in Chief of the armed forces. Before he would accept the post, however, Kornilov had demanded certain military reforms. Kerensky had agreed, but had put off implementing them.

A former Provisional Government official who, up to that time, had been a minor player in revolutionary intrigue, emerged to unwittingly save the day for the Bolsheviks. Vladimir Lvov, in a complicated mix-up of messages between Kerensky and Kornilov, managed to convince both men that each was about to betray the other and make himself dictator. If the long-term results were not so tragic, the back-and-forth messages would have been comical. But what did result was that Kerensky, though he became aware that Kornilov had also been misled, relieved him of his command and charged him with treason. Kerensky then asked the Bolsheviks for their help. Forty thousand guns were given out to workers, to stave off Kornilov's supposed military takeover. The majority of these guns became the basic arsenal of the Bolshevik Red Guards.

Instead of increasing his authority within the government, however, the Kornilov affair cut off Kerensky from any future military help. Since it appeared that Kornilov, given his views on the ineffectiveness of the government, might have tried a takeover, the officers of the garrison would not get involved to help Kerensky. They felt that Kornilov had been treated unjustly. Kerensky's days as a leader were numbered.

Lenin by Letter

Lenin and Grigori Zinoviev, disguised as farm laborers in Finland, kept up with the news from Russia through secret messengers. Though dispirited by the failure of the July demonstrations to turn into a complete overthrow of the government, Lenin kept up his writing. In addition to articles and letters, he worked on a book he had begun in Switzerland. It was called *State and Revolution.*

When he heard about the Kornilov-Kerensky mess in which Kerensky was actually helping to arm the Bolsheviks, Lenin's mood improved greatly.[1] By September, when Leon Trotsky became chairman of the Petrograd Soviet, Bolshevik power was on the upswing. Trotsky advocated using a nationwide organization of Soviets, in which Bolsheviks held power. This would be done for the sole purpose of seizing control of all the other Soviets, including that of Petrograd.[2] Again, the Bolsheviks were split over their readiness to bring this about.

By way of letter from Finland, Lenin urged, "the Bolsheviks can and must seize power."[3] Trotsky, too, was in favor of swift movement. Kamenev and Zinoviev voted against an overly quick move. They said it would risk the party, as well as the Russian and world revolutions.[4]

Lenin was infuriated. He saw anyone who opposed his revolutionary goals as an enemy. He wanted Kamenev and Zinoviev expelled from the party because of their dissenting opinion. In 1902, Lenin had proclaimed, "give us an organization of revolutionaries and we will overturn Russia."[5] Nothing had changed.

The rest of the party leadership, however, did not see the need or the sense of immediate action. Russia was still involved in World War I, though few soldiers remained at the front. The Provisional Government

Source Document

The situation is critical in the extreme. In fact it is now absolutely clear that to delay the uprising would be fatal.

With all my might I urge comrades to realize that everything now hangs by a thread; that we are confronted by problems which are not to be solved by conferences or congresses (even congresses of Soviets), but exclusively by peoples, by the masses, by the struggle of the armed people. . . .

We must not wait! We may lose everything! . . .

History will not forgive revolutionaries for procrastinating when they could be victorious today (and they certainly will be victorious today), while they risk losing much tomorrow, in fact, they risk losing everything.

If we seize power today, we seize it not in opposition to the Soviets but on their behalf.

The seizure of power is the business of the uprising; its political purpose will become clear after the seizure. . . .

The government is tottering. It must be given the death-blow at all costs.[6]

Lenin made this statement, urging his fellow revolutionaries to take their opportunity to overthrow the Russian government.

still had commitments to the Allies. A meeting, or congress, of the various Soviets was soon to take place. The Bolsheviks could use the Soviets to assume power peacefully.

Lenin exploded. In letters he asked: What if the government surrendered Petrograd to the Germans? What if the elections, scheduled by the government to be held on November 12, resulted in an actual democratic election of revolutionaries? How, then, could the Bolsheviks continue to act for the people—as Lenin believed they must—when the people had already elected for themselves?[7]

Once again, Lenin had to back down and wait. But the Bolsheviks did not waver or act confused—however confused they may have been. As anarchy in the country increased, the Petrograd Soviet did not try to prevent the Bolsheviks from having time to gather pro-Bolshevik delegates for the congress of Soviets. The congress quickly focused on gaining approval for a Bolshevik coup.

The Defense of the Capital

Germany had completed a naval operation that occupied three islands close to Petrograd. Russians now wondered if the capital should move to Moscow, which was farther inland. The Bolshevik Soviets did not want this, because it might help to strengthen the Provisional Government. When it was decided that the government would remain in Petrograd, the Bolsheviks offered their military services for the defense of the capital. As the only military unit not controlled by the Provisional Government, this would put the Bolsheviks in control.

By this time, Lenin had resurfaced in Petrograd. This was extremely dangerous for him, but he did not trust that other Bolsheviks would act swiftly, decisively, and at the correct time without his being there to help direct their actions. Lenin wanted a coup to occur immediately. Kamenev and Zinoviev thought it should come later. Trotsky and some others believed that the coup should occur in conjunction with the congress of Soviets that would take place on November 7.

Lenin's strategy was offensive, but it claimed to be defensive, hiding behind the excuse that the Germans were about to take over, so the Bolsheviks had to save the day.[8] The Provisional Government, as usual, used half measures in its effort to contain the Bolsheviks, exposing its own lack of unity and decisiveness. Though the government shut down several Bolshevik newspapers, it failed to stop growing Bolshevik military strength. Given power by the government, the Bolsheviks, in the name of the Soviet, had formed a military-revolutionary committee called the *Milrevkom*. This committee controlled only a minority of Petrograd's troops in October. By early November, however, the Milrevkom had enlisted a large number of other military units by convincing soldiers that they must defend the revolution against a weak government that might give in to the Germans.

These people are Bolsheviks, showing their support for the revolution.

Takeover

On the night of November 6–7, the Bolsheviks took over the city of Petrograd. Pickets were posted, and anyone who objected was disarmed. No violence occurred as the Milrevkom took over telephone and telegraph offices, banks, bridges, and railroad lines. Military staff headquarters became Bolshevik quarters. According to one participant, in the most casual manner imaginable "they [the Bolsheviks] entered and sat down while those who had been sitting there got up and left; thus the Staff was taken."[9]

Alexander Kerensky tried to get military backup to protect the Provisional Government at the Winter Palace but failed. He fled toward the war front the next morning. However, the Winter Palace was not yet Bolshevik territory, and Lenin wanted it to be captured. The evening had gone so smoothly that no troops could be seen. The few Bolsheviks who were willing to assault the Winter Palace retreated when they heard shots.

Nevertheless, Lenin, at party headquarters, proclaimed victory for the revolution of workers, soldiers, and peasants. He drafted a declaration that recognized "sovereign power over Russia to have been assumed by a body that no one except the Bolshevik Central Committee had authorized to do so."[10] Because there was no violence and the night had been virtually undisturbed, on the morning of November 7, people went on with their lives as usual.

Kerensky, from the war front, tried to get the army to restore order to Petrograd. Other forces got close to Petrograd, fired a few ineffectual shots, and stopped. The governmental cabinet, trapped in the Winter Palace, sat around waiting for help. Outside defenders, tired of waiting for reinforcements, drifted away.

There were still government troops and ministers of the Provisional Government in the Winter Palace. All that day, small groups of Bolsheviks entered the palace. They let themselves be disarmed by the bedraggled government troops while trying to convince them to join the Bolshevik cause. By 2:00 A.M. on November 8, Red Guard and sailor troops were able to storm the Winter Palace without firing a shot. The Bolsheviks, with nobody trying to stop them, entered the Winter Palace and arrested the members of the cabinet. In the small room where the ministers waited, a revolutionary named Vladimir Antonov-Ovseenko declared, "In the name of the Military and Revolutionary Committee of the Petrograd Soviet, I declare the Provisional Government deposed. All are arrested."[11] The former ministers were taken as prisoners to Peter and Paul Fortess.

Lenin's declaration of successful revolution was approved by the congress of Soviets, which met until dawn. Not everyone was happy about the Bolsheviks' success. The more moderate revolutionary delegates left the meeting to show their disapproval.

So far, the revolution had occurred without bloodshed. If not a total surprise to both the revolutionaries

Lenin is seen here (at right) in his office, discussing his plans for governing Russia.

themselves and to people of Petrograd, the revolution was at least unexpected in its scope and suddenness. It was so sudden, in fact, that few people thought it would last until the end of the year. Trotsky, writing later about the coup, said:

> If neither Lenin nor I had been present in Petersburg, there would have been no October Revolution [the coup took place in October rather than November on the old-style Russian calendar]: the leadership of the Bolshevik Party would have prevented it from occurring—of this I have not the slightest doubt! If Lenin had not been in Petersburg, I doubt whether I could have managed to conquer the resistance of the Bolshevik leaders.[12]

Whether the majority of the Bolshevik leadership had wanted it or not, a revolution had, in fact, occurred. "No one except a handful of principals," wrote historian Richard Pipes, "knew what had happened—that Petrograd was in the iron grip of armed Bolsheviks and nothing would ever be the same."[13]

Chapter 13

The Bolsheviks Govern

To think that managing this new state that used to be the Russian Empire would be as easy as storming the Winter Palace, was, of course, unrealistic. The Bolsheviks, and particularly their leader, Lenin, were experienced in revolutionary tactics, terrorism, and organizing—but not in government administration. What would they do now?

Setting Up a New Government

Bertrand Russell, a British philosopher, defined Bolshevism as "an impatient philosophy, which aims at creating a new world without sufficient preparation in the opinions and feelings of ordinary men and women."[1] It was the ordinary men, women, and children of Russia who would suffer to allow that ideology to succeed.

Source Document

By replacing private with public ownership of the means of production and exchange, by introducing planned organisation in the public process of production so that the well being and the many sided development of all members of society may be ensured, the social revolution of the proletariat will abolish the division of society into classes and thus emancipate all oppressed humanity, and will terminate all forms of exploitation of one part of society by another.

A necessary condition for this social revolution is the dictatorship of the proletariat; that is, the conquering by the proletariat of such political power as would enable it to crush any resistance offered by the exploiters. In its effort to make the proletariat capable of fulfilling its great historical mission, international social democracy organises it into an independent political party in opposition to all bourgeois parties, directs all the manifestations of its class struggle, discloses before it the irreconcilable conflict between the interests of the exploiters and those of the exploited, and clarifies for it the historical significance of the imminent social revolution and the conditions necessary for its coming.[2]

The Bolshevik party outlined its basic beliefs and plans for the government in this document.

The first thing the new Bolshevik leaders had to do was stop any threat that Alexander Kerensky could come back to Petrograd with enough army troops to stage a counter-coup. Kerensky was able to gather only a small force before he once again escaped, and finally went to America. There, he wrote and lectured, living to the age of eighty.

With Kerensky gone, there remained the problem of governing. First, the Bolsheviks wanted new names for the members of the government. The old term *ministers* was considered too much of a reminder of the old tsarist regime. Members of the government would now be called People's Commissars.[3] The government itself would be called the Soviet of People's Commissars. This suggestion was Trotsky's. Lenin liked it because it sounded revolutionary.[4]

Lenin was now the manager of this new government, which proposed to rule over 150 million Russians of varied class and ethnic backgrounds. As he led seemingly endless meetings, Lenin insisted that members of the *Sovnarkom*, the party cabinet, be on time and stick exactly to the time allotted for their speeches. Being tardy or absent resulted in punishment. Lenin himself worked constantly, as usual, but the tediousness of running a government was difficult for a man who, for years, had moved around from country to country, never having to follow a daily routine. He became continually tired.

Lenin worked to make sure state and local organizations were always under the tight control of the centralized government. According to historian Dmitri Volkogonov,

> The old state machine had been broken and the new one was primitive, inefficient and from its very inception markedly bureaucratic. Perhaps even Lenin did not then realize that the new structures being erected were in fact the foundations of a vast totalitarian system.[5]

The Government and Its Problems

Government agencies are usually headed by professionals who have experience in the area to be handled by the agency. Someone familiar with finance, for example, would become finance minister; someone who knew about agriculture would become the head of the agriculture department, and so forth. In the new system set up by the Bolsheviks, however, "class considerations took precedence over professionalism. . . ."[6] This created clumsy, inefficient, and often corrupt government. The military, too, became disorganized as a result of many of the same kinds of decisions.

Because the "dictatorship of the proletariat"—which was actually a dictatorship of the Bolshevik party—was more important than day-to-day details, government agencies were not monitored closely to make them more effective. Disorganization in the government led to terrible food shortages and breakdowns of all kinds of essential services throughout Russia. Pressed by liberal and social democratic groups—out of power but still in existence—to hold

Source Document

. . . Article 3. Its fundamental aim being abolition of all exploitation of man by man, complete elimination of the division of society into classes, merciless suppression of the exploiters, socialist organization of society, and victory of socialism in all countries, the Third All-Russia Congress of Soviets of Workers', Soldiers' and Peasants' Deputies further resolves:

a. Pursuant to the socialization of land, private land ownership is hereby abolished, and all land is proclaimed the property of the entire people. . . .

b. All forests, mineral wealth and waters of national importance, as well as all live and dead stock, model estates and agricultural enterprises are proclaimed the property of the nation.

c. The Soviet laws on workers' control and on the Supreme Economic Council are hereby confirmed in order to guarantee the power of the working people over the exploiters and as a first step towards the complete conversion of factories, mines, railways and other means of production and transportation into the property of the Soviet Workers' and Peasants' Republic. . . .

e. To ensure the sovereign power of the working people and to rule out any possibility of restoration of the power of the exploiters, the arming of the working people, the creation of a socialist Red Army of workers and peasants, and the complete disarming of the propertied classes are hereby decreed.[7]

The new Constitution adopted in 1918 showed the drastic steps the Soviets were taking toward creating a Communist nation.

elections for a Constituent Assembly, Lenin did so. However, when the Bolshevik party did not receive a majority of votes, Lenin simply did away with the Constituent Assembly, just as the tsar had done with the Duma in 1906 and 1907.

The Bolshevik government proceeded to mount a campaign of terror by creating the Extraordinary Commission to Combat Counter-Revolution and Sabotage (Cheka). This new agency was at least as ruthless as the tsar's secret police had been, and it served the same function. It took as prisoners those people who disagreed politically with the Bolsheviks, threatening to execute them if any Bolsheviks came to harm.

To make matters worse, once again, the peasants were starving. By the 1920s, between 7 million and 9 million children had been orphaned or abandoned because their parents had died or could no longer take care of them.

While trying to figure out how to run Russia, the Bolsheviks still had to deal with the pesky war. World War I was threatening to enter Russia once again. Although Lenin had declared neutrality and an armistice, neither Russia's allies nor its enemies paid much attention. No one but the Germans seemed pleased that the Reds—a name for the Bolsheviks taken from their use of the color red as a symbol—had been unleashed in Russia. While the Allies helped Russian troops against German troops, they also helped counterrevolutionary, or White, troops mobilize to fight against the Bolsheviks. Soon a full-scale civil war was raging in the country. It became apparent to Lenin that World War I, at least for Russia, must be ended.

The Treaty of Brest-Litovsk

Making peace with Germany proved even more humiliating to the Russians than losing Chinese Manchuria to the Japanese had been. The Treaty of Brest-Litovsk, signed in March 1918 between Russia and Germany, forced Russia to give up a quarter of its territory. This area included the Baltic States, Poland, the Ukraine, part of Byelorussia, and land bordering Turkey. One third of Russia's population, as well as many farms and industries, were located in these areas.

Lenin had no intention of honoring all the treaty's terms. He also hoped, since world revolution was his ultimate aim, that Germany would revolt against its monarchy and join the Bolshevik cause. In the meantime, he was satisfied to have Russia out of the war. The government moved to Moscow, farther away from possible German attack, taking up headquarters in the walled Kremlin, from which tsars had ruled in the medieval past.

The Revolution Turns Violent

Violence reigned in the countryside. Bolsheviks were being assassinated by counterrevolutionaries. They, in turn, were killed by Bolsheviks. The new government

The Kremlin, seen here as it looks today, was the center of government from tsarist times through the years of Communist rule.

quickly became as hated and feared as the tsars' had been.

One of the worst tragedies of 1918 was the murder of Tsar Nicholas II and his entire family on July 17. They had been moved to Yekaterinburg, where some former members of the Provisional Government hoped to keep them safe. Fearing the tsar would be a symbol for those who opposed the Bolsheviks to rally around, the party decided it was best to eliminate Nicholas, as well as his wife and children. The entire family was brutally shot and killed in the basement of the house in which they had been staying. Nervous

Tsar Nicholas II (center) and his family. Clockwise from far left, daughters Maria, Olga, Tatiana, and Anastasia; son, Alexis; and wife, Alexandra.

about public reaction, the Bolsheviks leaked the false story that only the tsar had been shot and the rest of the family had been sent away. Perhaps this marked the defining moment at which the Bolshevik Revolution became a force that was willing to ignore human suffering in pursuit of its goals.

Perhaps the revolution can best be summed up in the words of writer Maxim Gorky, once an ardent believer in Lenin and the revolution. In an essay called "Triumph Disappointed," Gorky told of a conversation with an old revolutionary who had told him about a dream he had had:

> Now that I am wide awake I can still see the triumphant people, but I feel that I am a stranger among them. . . . Maybe I, like many others, do not know how to triumph. All my energy went in the struggle; the expectation, the capacity for enjoying possession; is stunted. . . . the point is that I see lots of ferocity and revenge about me, but never any joy—the joy that transfigures a man. And I do not see any faith in victory. . . . I feel utterly miserable—just as Columbus would have felt if he had reached the coast of America only to find that it was repulsive to him.[8]

Chapter 14

Lenin's Legacy

In 1918, two attempts were made on Lenin's life. One, on January 14, came as shots were fired at his car as it traveled to Bolshevik headquarters in Moscow. Lenin was uninjured in the incident, but on August 30, as he was giving a speech at a factory, he was shot twice at point-blank range by a young revolutionary named Fanny Kaplan. One bullet entered his lungs near the heart, and the other his left shoulder near the neck. Characteristically, Lenin tried to make light of the injuries he suffered.

Rumors flew that he was dead, but he actually recovered faster than was expected. Before she was executed, Fanny Kaplan explained why she had tried to assassinate Lenin. She said she believed he was a traitor to the revolution, and would put the cause of socialism back many years.[1]

After this attempt on his life, Lenin became even more revered by Bolsheviks and their supporters. Terrorist reprisals against "enemies of the state" increased. Full-scale civil war was soon to follow.

The Death of Lenin

Lenin lived only five more years after this assassination attempt. He suffered a series of strokes that steadily diminished first his physical strength, then his speech. He tried desperately to maintain control over party affairs right up until his third and last stroke. Lenin died on Monday, January 21, 1924.

"The Party leaders saw in the very act of Lenin's burial an enormous opportunity for strengthening the regime," wrote historian Dmitri Volkogonov.[2] At first, Lenin was simply to be buried after a state ceremony. However, a new procedure that mummified bodies (preserved the flesh) had recently been discovered. It was decided to preserve Lenin's body for permanent display to the public. This grisly idea soon took hold, and a huge mausoleum was built in the Kremlin so that Communists could make a pilgrimage to see the legendary leader of the new order.

A Scramble for Power

Before Lenin's death, power had been passing to a handful of top Bolsheviks who were trusted by Lenin: Joseph Stalin was the party administrator; Lev Kamenev managed Moscow; Zinoviev managed Petrograd; and Leon Trotsky dealt with the army, but

A crowd gathered at Lenin's tomb to honor the fallen leader of the Russian Revolution.

never having been fully accepted by the Bolsheviks, he fell from power not long after Lenin's death.

Although it took a few years for him to emerge as the party's undisputed leader, by 1927, Joseph Stalin had taken over Lenin's position as the dictator of the Union of Soviet Socialist Republics (USSR), the new name for Communist Russia. Stalin had been very clever at hiding his ruthlessness during his early years as a party leader. Still, before this death, Lenin had begun to distrust him and warned party leaders not to give

Source Document

This, of course, does not mean that the October uprising did not have its inspirer. It did have its inspirer and leader, but this was Lenin, and none other than Lenin, that same Lenin whose resolutions the Central Committee adopted when deciding the question of the uprising, that same Lenin who, in spite of what Trotsky says, was not prevented by being in hiding from being the actual inspirer of the uprising. It is foolish and ridiculous to attempt now, by gossip about Lenin having been in hiding, to obscure the indubitable fact that the inspirer of the uprising was the leader of the Party, V. I. Lenin.

Such are the facts. . . .

[I]t cannot be denied that Trotsky fought well in the period of October. Yes, that is true, Trotsky did, indeed, fight well in October; but Trotsky was not the only one who fought well in the period of October. Even people like the Left Socialist-Revolutionaries, who then stood side by side with the Bolsheviks, also fought well. In general, I must say that in the period of a victorious uprising, when the enemy is isolated and the uprising is growing, it is not difficult to fight well. At such moments even backward people become heroes.[3]

Stalin defended Lenin as the main leader of the Russian Revolution in this speech he delivered in November 1924.

Stalin great power. Lenin's final stroke so incapacitated him, however, that he was unable to do anything to dilute Stalin's power.

The dream of socialist equality passed, therefore, into the hands of Joseph Stalin. Like Lenin, Stalin believed consistently through his life that the final goal of Marxism—equality for all classes—justified any means to reach that end. This included the mass terror that Lenin had started and that Stalin brought into full being. By the end of Stalin's regime, the USSR would

Joseph Stalin (right), who was one of Lenin's chief advisors during the early days of the Soviet Union, eventually rose to become the dictator of the nation.

This poster honoring the Russian Revolution portrays Lenin (left) as the fearless leader of the Soviet people.

be a nation marked by repression, censorship, and violence against those the government deemed a threat. It was Lenin, with his genuinely admirable qualities of courage, determination, intelligence, and single-mindedness, who "helped to inaugurate . . . a system of life unacceptable to those outside the mental and physical strait-jacket of Communist beliefs."[4]

Today, we know that the USSR, the world superpower that grew out of the Russian Revolution, has now been dissolved. Years of financial troubles and the increasing desire of the people for greater freedom caused the fall of the Soviet system in the late 1980s. Russia is currently experiencing even more difficulties. As Lenin had learned when he and the Bolsheviks replaced the Provisional Government and the tsarist system, creating change in an orderly and humane way is a terribly difficult task.

As Russia enters a new millennium, the people's wish for a more democratic nation has not yet been completely fulfilled. Much work remains to be done to overcome the legacy of Lenin and the Russian Revolution.

Timeline

All dates are new-style.

1870—*April 22*: Lenin (Vladimir Ilych Ulyanov) born in Simbirsk, Russia.

1881—*March 13*: Tsar Alexander II assassinated.

1886—*January 24*: Lenin's father dies.

1887—*May 20*: Lenin's brother, Alexander Ulyanov, executed.
August 25: Lenin enters Kazan University.
December 17: Lenin arrested for participation in a student protest demonstration.

1891—Lenin passes law examination at St. Petersburg University.

1892—Lenin works as a lawyer in Samara.

1895—*May–September*: Lenin travels abroad and meets Georgi Plekhanov.
December 21: Lenin arrested in St. Petersburg.

1897—*February 10*: Lenin starts three-year exile in Siberia.

1898—*March*: Russian Social Democratic Labor party (RSDLP) founded in Minsk, Russia.
July 22: Lenin marries Nadezhda Krupskaya in Shushenskoe, Siberia.

1900—*February 10*: Lenin's exile ends.
March: Lenin arrives in St. Petersburg.
June 3: Lenin is arrested but is released ten days later.

June 29: Lenin leaves Russia to go to Western Europe.

1902—*March*: Lenin's *What Is to Be Done?* published.

1903—*July–August*: Second congress of RSDLP is held in Brussels and London; At it, the Bolshevik and Menshevik factions split.

1904—*February*: Beginning of Russo-Japanese War.

1905—*January 22*: "Bloody Sunday" takes place in St. Petersburg.
September 5: Peace treaty with Japan signed in Portsmouth, New Hampshire.
October 30: Manifesto signed by Nicholas II, promising civil rights and the Duma.
November 21: Lenin arrives in St. Petersburg.

1906—*May 10*: First Duma opens in St. Petersburg.
July 21: First Duma dissolved; Pëtr Stolypin is appointed prime minister.

1907—*January–April*: Lenin lives in Finland.
December: Lenin moves to Switzerland.

1908—*December*: Lenin moves to Paris, France.

1911—Stolypin assassinated.

1912—*June*: Lenin moves to Poland.

1914—*July 30*: Russia prepares for war with Germany.
August 1: Germany declares war on Russia.
August 3: World War I begins.
August 8: Lenin arrested in Austrian Poland.
August 19: Lenin released.
September: Lenin leaves for Switzerland.

1915—*September*: Tsar Nicholas II takes over as commander of Russian forces.

1916—*December 30*: Rasputin murdered in Petrograd.

1917—*March 8*: February Revolution begins in Petrograd.
March 12: Formation of Petrograd Soviet.
March 15: Provisional Government formed; Nicholas II abdicates.
April 16: Lenin arrives in Petrograd.
May: Bolshevik Red Guard formed.
November 6: Bolshevik Red Guards take over Petrograd.
December 20: Cheka established.

1918—*January 14*: Assassination attempt on Lenin.
March 3: Treaty of Brest-Litovsk signed between Russia and Germany.
July 17: Tsar Nicholas II and his family are murdered.

1922—*April*: Stalin becomes General Secretary of the Communist party.

1924—*January 21*: Lenin dies.

Chapter Notes

Chapter 1. Revolution!

1. Dmitri Volkogonov, *Lenin, A New Biography* (New York: The Free Press, 1994), p. 106.

2. Richard Pipes, *A Concise History of the Russian Revolution* (New York: Alfred A. Knopf, 1995), p. 114.

3. Ronald W. Clark, *Lenin, A Biography* (New York: Harper and Row, 1988), pp. 191–207.

Chapter 2. Who Was Lenin?

1. Dmitri Volkogonov, *Lenin, A New Biography* (New York: The Free Press, 1994), p. 5.

2. Robert Payne, *The Life and Death of Lenin* (New York: Simon & Schuster, 1964), p. 46.

3. Ibid., p. 50.

4. Volkogonov, p. 11.

5. Payne, p. 48.

6. Ibid., p. 49.

7. Ronald W. Clark, *Lenin, A Biography* (New York: Harper and Row, 1988), p. 11.

8. Ibid.

9. Volkogonov, p. 12.

10. Payne, p. 52; Clark, p. 10.

11. Clark, p. 14.

Chapter 3. Groundwork for Revolution

1. Bertram D. Wolfe, *Three Who Made A Revolution* (Boston: Beacon Press, 1948), p. 18.

2. Richard Pipes, *A Concise History of the Russian Revolution* (New York: Alfred A. Knopf, 1995), p. 14.

3. Ibid., p. 4.

4. From *Polnoe sobranie zakonov Russkoi Imperii (Complete Collection of the Laws of the Russian Empire)*, 2nd series, vol. 36, no. 36490, pp. 130–134.

5. W. Bruce Lincoln, *In War's Dark Shadow* (New York, Cambridge: The Dial Press, 1983), p. 50.

6. Wolfe, p. 64.

Chapter 4. The Making of a Revolutionary

1. Dmitri Volkogonov, *Lenin, A New Biography* (New York: The Free Press, 1994), p. 18.

2. Ibid., p. 19.

3. Karl Marx, "Capital, Volume One," *The Marx-Engels Reader*, 2nd ed., ed. Robert C. Tucker (New York: W. W. Norton & Company, 1978), p. 326.

4. Karl Marx and Friedrich Engels, "Manifesto of the Communist Party," *The Marx-Engels Reader*, 2nd ed., ed. Robert C. Tucker (New York: W. W. Norton & Company, 1978), p. 500.

5. Harold Shukman, *Lenin and the Russian Revolution* (New York: Capricorn Books, 1968), pp. 25–26.

6. Elyse Topalian, *V. I. Lenin* (New York: Franklin Watts, 1983), p. 28.

7. Bertram D. Wolfe, *Three Who Made A Revolution* (Boston: Beacon Press, 1948), p. 85.

8. W. Bruce Lincoln, *In War's Dark Shadow* (New York, Cambridge: The Dial Press, 1983), pp. 18–19.

9. G. V. Plekhanov, *The Role of the Individual in History*, n. d., <http://art-bin.com/art/oplecheng.html>.

10. Volkogonov, p. 27.

11. Ibid., pp. 26, 27.

Chapter 5. In Siberia

1. Harold Shukman, *Lenin and the Russian Revolution* (New York: Capricorn Books, 1968), p. 43.

2. Dmitri Volkogonov, *Lenin, A New Biography* (New York: The Free Press, 1994), p. 24.

3. Richard Pipes, *A Concise History of the Russian Revolution* (New York: Alfred A. Knopf, 1995), p. 31.

4. Volkogonov, pp. 31–32.

5. Ronald W. Clark, *Lenin, A Biography* (New York: Harper and Row, 1988), p. 32.

6. Ibid., p. 34.

7. Henry M. Christman, ed., *Essential Works of Lenin: "What Is to Be Done?" and Other Writings* (New York: Dover Publications, Inc., 1987), p. 148.

8. Pipes, p. 106.

Chapter 6. Solidifying Leadership

1. Robert Service, *Lenin: A Biography* (Cambridge, Mass.: The Belknap Press of Harvard University Press, 2000), p. 135.

2. Bertram D. Wolfe, *Three Who Made A Revolution* (Boston: Beacon Press, 1948), p. 145.

3. Ibid., p. 146.

4. Ibid., p. 145.

5. Service, pp. 132–133.

6. Dmitri Volkogonov, *Lenin, A New Biography* (New York: The Free Press, 1994), p. 1.

7. Ibid., p. 50.

8. Ibid., p. 55.

Chapter 7. Bloody Sunday and Its Aftermath

1. Richard Pipes, *A Concise History of the Russian Revolution* (New York: Alfred A. Knopf, 1995), p. 35.

2. Robert Service, *Lenin: A Biography* (Cambridge, Mass.: The Belknap Press of Harvard University Press, 2000), p. 167.

3. Pipes, p. 39.

4. Ronald W. Clark, *Lenin, A Biography* (New York: Harper and Row, 1988), pp. 101–102.

5. Pipes, p. 40.

6. Ibid., p. 41.

7. Ibid., p. 42.

8. *Polnoe sobranie zakonov Rossiiskoi Imperii (Complete Collection of the Laws of the Russian Empire)*, 3rd series, vol. XXVI, no. 26803.

Chapter 8. The Bolsheviks and Mensheviks

1. Harold Shukman, *Lenin and the Russian Revolution* (New York: Capricorn Books, 1968), p. 79.

2. Ibid., p. 81.

3. Ibid.

4. Bertram D. Wolfe, *Three Who Made A Revolution* (Boston: Beacon Press, 1948), p. 335.

5. Shukman, p. 81.

6. Robert Service, *Lenin: A Biography* (Cambridge, Mass.: The Belknap Press of Harvard University Press, 2000), pp. 169–170.

7. V. I. Lenin, *Selected Works* (Moscow: Progress Publishers, 1975), vol. 1, pp. 529–534.

8. Service, pp. 178–179.

Chapter 9. World War I

1. Elise Topalian, *V. I. Lenin* (New York: Franklin Watts, 1983), p. 78.

2. Dmitri Volkogonov, *Lenin, A New Biography* (New York: The Free Press, 1994), p. 105.

3. Bertram D. Wolfe, *Three Who Made A Revolution* (Boston: Beacon Press, 1948), p. 53.

Chapter 10. The Fall of the Tsar

1. Richard Pipes, *A Concise History of the Russian Revolution* (New York: Alfred A. Knopf, 1995), p. 77.

2. Elise Topalian, *V. I. Lenin* (New York: Franklin Watts, 1983), p. 82.

3. Richard Pipes, *A Concise History of the Russian Revolution* (New York: Alfred A. Knopf, 1995), p. 80.

4. Ibid., p. 81.

5. Ibid., pp. 82–83.

6. Ibid., p. 84.

7. *The Times*, March 19, 1917, <http://www.dur.ac.uk/~dml0www/abdicatn.html>.

8. Pipes, p. 80.

Chapter 11. The Return of Lenin

1. Dmitri Volkogonov, *Lenin, A New Biography* (New York: The Free Press, 1994), p. 121.

2. Ronald W. Clark, *Lenin, A Biography* (New York: Harper and Row, 1988), p. 210; Volkogonov, p. 140.

3. Richard Pipes, *A Concise History of the Russian Revolution* (New York: Alfred A. Knopf, 1995), p. 117.

4. Harold Shukman, *Lenin and the Russian Revolution* (New York: Capricorn Books, 1968), p. 178.

5. Pipes, p. 115.

6. Ibid., p. 120.

7. Volkogonov, p. 139.

8. Pipes, p. 127.

9. Volkogonov, p. 140.

Chapter 12. The October Coup

1. Richard Pipes, *A Concise History of the Russian Revolution* (New York: Alfred A. Knopf, 1995), p. 136.

2. Ibid.

3. Ibid., p. 137.

4. Harold Shukman, *Lenin and the Russian Revolution* (New York: Capricorn Books, 1968), p. 192.

5. Ibid., p. 183.

6. Paul Halsall, "Lenin: Call to Power, Oct 24, 1917," *Modern History Sourcebook*, August 1997, <http://www.fordham.edu/halsall/mod/modsbook39.html>.

7. Pipes, p. 139.

8. Ibid., pp. 139–140.

9. Ibid., p. 145.

10. Ibid.

11. Ronald W. Clark, *Lenin, A Biography* (New York: Harper and Row, 1988), pp. 272–273.

12. Ibid., pp. 274–275.

13. Pipes, p. 146.

Chapter 13. The Bolsheviks Govern

1. Harold Shukman, *Lenin and the Russian Revolution* (New York: Capricorn Books, 1968), p. 8.

2. R. C. Elwood, ed., *Resolutions and Decisions of the Communist Party of the Soviet Union, The Russian Social Democratic Labour Party, 1898–October 1917* (Toronto: n. p., 1974), vol. 1, pp. 42–45.

3. Dmitri Volkogonov, *Lenin, A New Biography* (New York: The Free Press, 1994), p. 162.

4. Ibid., p. 163.

5. Ibid., p. 167.

6. Ibid., p. l66.

7. Robert Beard, *Constitution (Fundamental Law) of the RSFSR*, 1996, <http://coral.bucknell.edu/departments/russian/const/18cons01.html#chap01>.

8. Maxim Gorky, "Triumph Disappointed," *Fragments from My Diary* (Middlesex, England: Penguin Books, 1972), p. 199.

Chapter 14. Lenin's Legacy

1. Dmitri Volkogonov, *Lenin, A New Biography* (New York: The Free Press, 1994), p. 224.

2. Ibid., p. 436.

3. Carl Kavanagh, *Trotskyism or Leninism? by J. V. Stalin*, n.d., <http://csf.colorado.edu/psn/marx/Other/Stalin/Archive/1924-tro.htm>.

4. Ronald W. Clark, *Lenin, A Biography* (New York: Harper and Row, 1988), p. 494.

Further Reading

Clark, Ronald W. *Lenin, A Biography.* New York: Harper & Row, 1988.

Figes, Orlando. *A People's Tragedy: A History of the Russian Revolution.* New York: Viking Penguin Books, 1996.

Pipes, Richard. *A Concise History of the Russian Revolution.* New York: Alfred A. Knopf, 1995.

Resnick, Abraham. *Lenin: Founder of the Soviet Union.* Chicago: Children's Press, 1987.

Service, Robert. *Lenin: A Biography.* Cambridge, Mass.: The Belknap Press of Harvard University Press, 2000.

Topalian, Elise. *V. I. Lenin.* New York: Franklin Watts, 1983.

Wade, Rex A. *The Russian Revolution, 1917.* New York, Cambridge: Cambridge University Press, 2000.

Internet Addresses

Canadian Forces College, Department of National Defence (Canada). *Military History: Russian Revolution (1917–1921)*. 1996–1998. <http://www.cfcsc.dnd.ca/links/milhist/rusrev.html>.

Halsall, Paul. "Russian Revolution Sourcebook." *Modern History Sourcebook*. August 1997. <http://www.fordham.edu/halsall/mod/modsbook39.html>.

Lenin Internet Archive. n.d. <http://www.marxists.org/archive/lenin/index.htm>.

Russia.net. "Revolutionary Times." *History*. n.d. <http://www.russia.net/history/revolution.html>.

Index